The Time I Lost My Mind But Found Myself

The Time I Lost My Mind But Found Myself

Kristina Joi Avant

ISBN 978-1-257-86719-6

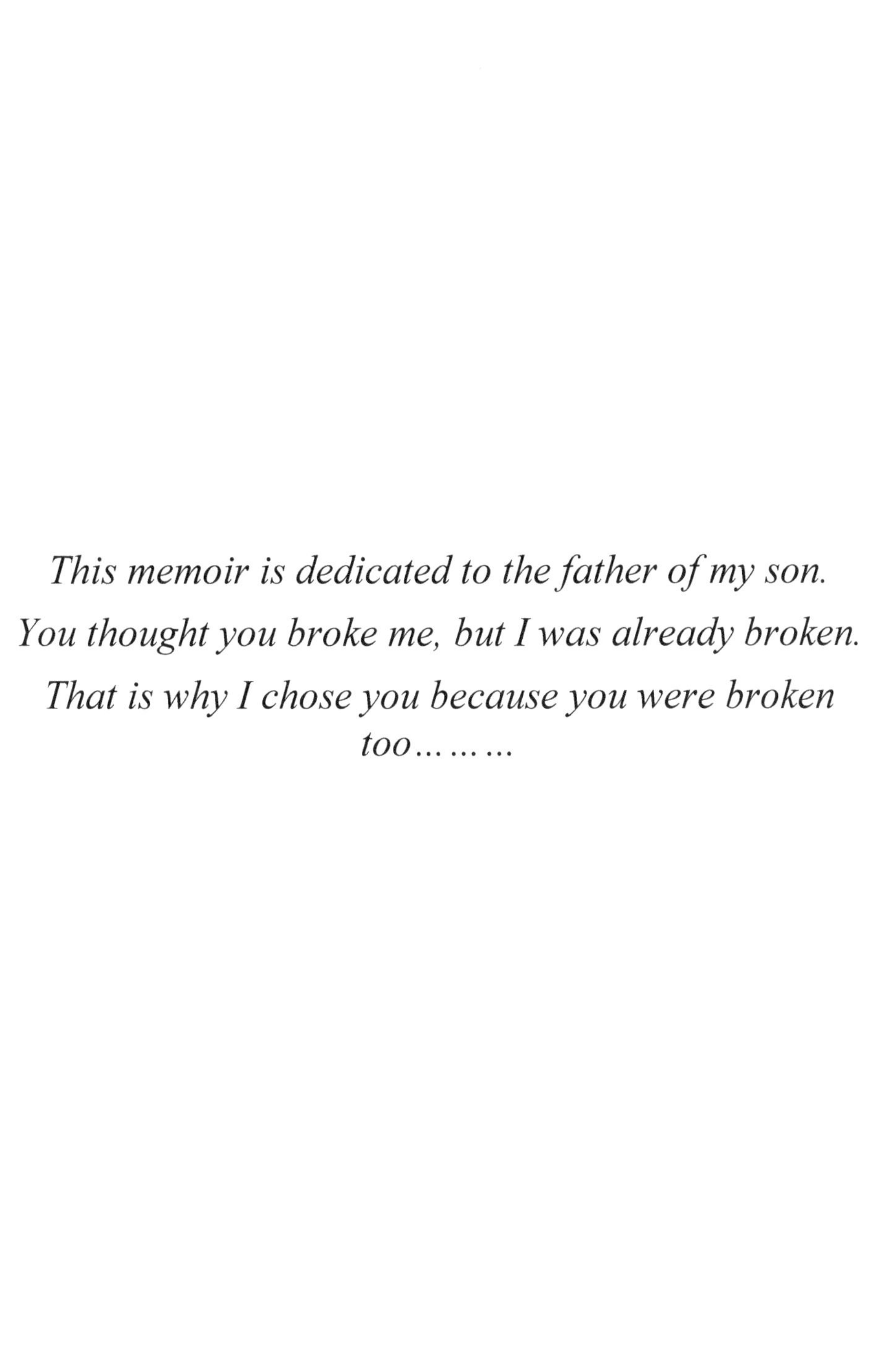

This memoir is dedicated to the father of my son.

You thought you broke me, but I was already broken.

That is why I chose you because you were broken too………

Thanks

First and foremost to my son and motivation, Styles Christian Avant-Pinkston, unlike most children you will have a reference book as to why your mother is so crazy. When it gets to be too much, remember I love you and it is all for you.

To all of my family and friends who encouraged me to write throughout my lifetime: Bobbie Avant, Rebecca Reese, Melinda Gale Reese, Clarice Carpenter, Tasia Pearson, Turiya Cobb, Nicole Askew, Adrian Dancy, Kwame Amoukou, Tom Popp, and Mariah Smyth.

To the Lulu staff for helping me make one of my dreams come true.

One

“This is Stan. Leave a message or page me. One.” I pressed end and then pressed talk. The phone rang for five times then as soon as I heard *This is Stan* I hit end again, and then talk. I repeated the synchronized button pushing for ten times before he picked up the phone.

“What!” Stan had finally picked up the phone, but I almost hung up anticipating his voicemail. “I’m taking the pills now so you better come and get Styles unless you want him to see his mother commit suicide.”, I said taunting him. He hung up. I pushed the talk button again.

He answered on the second ring, “If you kill yourself me and Styles won’t be at your funeral.”

“What do I care; I’ll be dead.” I chuckled as I picked up a small, white Claritin pill off of the floor. Stan had knocked all sixty pills out of the bottle in my hand before he left. There was a small knock at the bathroom door. “Mommy. Mommy, I have to pee.”

“Styles go away!” I yelled at the locked bathroom door, “See your son needs a stable parent so you better come and get him before I traumatize him for life.”

“Kristina, stop calling me with this bullshit.”

“You don’t care about anybody. You don’t care if I kill myself and you don’t care if our son is a witness to it. All you care about is running the fucking streets so you can drink and smoke with some niggers and fuck some hoes.” I yelled through the cell phone’s speaker.

“Mommy! What’s wrong?” Styles whined on the other side of the bathroom door.

"You're the mutherfucker who doesn't care about anyone. I'm not in the bathroom trying to kill myself." Stan hollered in my ear before he hung up again.

I was like a programmed robot. I kept pushing talk and then when his voicemail came on I pressed end, then repeat. I lost count after twenty. I wondered why the idiot just wouldn't turn his phone off, but then I realized he was probably on the other line with some bitch.

I threw the phone down and screamed. It separated into three pieces when it hit the ground; the front part, battery, and back part. Phones had been the cause of all this mess in the first place. Some girl had called Stan at three o' clock on Wednesday. According to him it was someone he had met before we got back together and he didn't understand why she was calling him so late. I was silent but my inside voice was telling me if it looks like a duck, quacks like a duck, then it is a duck. *That's probably who he was on the phone with now.* I screamed again until I thought my voice chords would shatter. Tiny rivers were flowing down my face. "Mommy! Mommy! Mommy!" Styles was crying too.

That Thursday I was on my way to work, still thinking about the three a.m. call girl when *he* appeared. *He* pulled up next to my dirty 1992 Geo Prism in a shiny white Escalade with silver rims that continued to spin even though the car was in park. I was blasting *Crazy in Love* on my CD player. "Hey Beyonce", he said. I turned my head to the left ready to give whoever this guy was an attitude for a couple of reasons: one because I was still pissed about the phone situation with Stan and two for interrupting me when I was listening to my song. When *Crazy in Love* came on I went into a trance. I really thought I was Beyonce and the beat hypnotized my ass. I could be talking to the Pope and the Dali Lama about world peace, but if *Crazy in Love* came on I would push them out of the way so I could do the 'uh oh uh oh uh oh' dance.

He melted the tip of my iceberg saying hey Beyonce. Even though I'm not a car groupie, when I saw this truck that could be in a rap video I got nicer. Then I saw *him*. *He* was gorgeous. I'm not the one to flip out over a guy, but here was my ideal man in the car next to me. I could hear that Roberta Flack song that my mother would always sing, *the first time I ever saw your face*. *He* was the color of Hershey's chocolate bars with perfect teeth the color of white keys on a baby grand piano. *His* lips were made for kissing, soft and plump. The shape of *his* head was perfect for his bald head. If I could use only one word to describe him I would use Maya Angelou's voice to say smooth. His skin, lips, head, and style were soooooo smooth. *He* reminded me of the model Tyson, but only in features. *He* was no pretty boy model with waxes, facials, and manicures. This was pure 100% man. A cliché had just pulled up next to me: tall, dark, and handsome.

Before I knew it I had parked my car, exchanged numbers with him, and taken a picture of him next to his truck with my new camera phone. I told him it was so his picture would come up when he called but it was really for proof for my girls. Guys like him didn't talk to girls like me. As he took my number, these girls walked by rolling their eyes out of jealousy. I could not help but gets that feeling that a girl must have when she is crowned homecoming queen or when a guy gets on bended knee to put a ring on her finger. That chosen feeling, that there were a lot of people but I wanted you feeling. He was the best of the best so made me feel like I was the best of best. I was so glad I had taken some time getting dressed that day, which was really pointless since I had to change into a tuxedo to waitress at the club I worked.

I did look like a fake Beyonce with my knee high replica Manolo Blahnik Timberland heels. I wore army fatigue short shorts with a white fitted tee topped off with a white Kango hat. Greg, that was his name, was doing a good impression of Jay-Z with t-shirt portraying Al Pacino as Scarface, expensive designer jeans, and all white Air Force Ones with black detailing. His chain, earring, and watch were real white gold and diamonds. Working in a jewelry store for two years had taught me to distinguish rhinestones from diamonds. Greg was a ghetto prince charming and I wanted to be his princess. I wanted him to save me with kiss and wake me up from my bad dream.

I did not think about Stan until I was back in the car driving to work. What if Greg called? But how could Stan trip when he was getting three a.m. booty calls? Besides, I thought, Greg was not going to call. I was a waitress at a member's only club. I served people with his type of money. I had a baby and I was still in college. I was sure that Greg had a stable of women without kids, good jobs, cars made in this decade, and more attractive. I parked my car at the parking lot across the street from the Sears Tower thinking, *'He is not going to call.'*

How wrong I had been, because Greg did call. He called on a rainy Sunday before Labor Day right after Stan and I finished having sex. When that *Crazy in Love* ringtone came on Stan would usually ignore it. If I wasn't in the room, he would yell to let me I had a call and I would return the same courtesy if his cell phone rang. I guess he was still light headed from busting a nut all over me because he picked up my phone to hand it to me. Since I took Greg's picture and programmed it in my phone, not only did his name appear but the screen showed him next to his truck too. It must have dropped a nuclear bomb on Stan's male ego. I could not help but feel pure happiness for making him feel how I had felt the Wednesday morning as I lay next to him in bed hearing another female's voice. I thought he would handle it like I did; be mad but hold it inside. "I ran into my ex", I tried to explain. Stan was not buying the bullshit I was trying to sell.

He just wanted to leave. That infuriated me. I saw bloody roses red. I had been understanding when the girl had called last Wednesday at three o'clock in the morning. Why was I not getting that same fairness? We had promised to spend all of Sunday together instead of going out with our friends to party for Labor Day weekend. Stan worked Monday thru Friday from nine to five, but my erratic schedule of going to school and working long hours as a catering waitress Monday thru Saturday made Sunday the only day we could spend together. Also it gave me a chance to catch my breath.

I got flashes in my head of him dancing on some girl in the club while I was in the house with Styles. Then memories replayed in my mind of my father leaving us almost every night to party with other women while my mother would yell at us because we were there and my father was not. I could remember thinking, *why does she let him do that? I will never let a man do that to me. I won't be anybody's doormat. No man will just leave me like I don't matter.* I watched Stan iron his clothes. My books for school were on the chest behind him. The bold black and red book for my black revolutionaries' class became my focus because it hurt to look at Stan. I thought of Nat Turner, Marcus Garvey, The Black Panthers, and of course Malcolm X. I wasn't going down without a fight. I thought to myself, *by any means necessary I was not letting Stan leave me.*

I put the phone back together and turned it back on. I dialed Stan's number again. To my surprise he picked up. I just knew he had turned the phone off by now. I could hear my M.O.P CD playing loud in the background. "What?" he asked in an annoyed tone.

Mrs. Marshall, my drama teacher at Notre Dame High School for Girls, would have been proud of me. She taught me to visualize images to portray a specific feeling to come through your acting. I pictured fog in the early morning. In my groggiest voice I said, "I think you have to come back. (Sigh) I don't feel well. I took the whole bottle of pills."

"How many did you take?" Urgency was in his voice and he had turned his music down. I could not stop a smile from forming on my lips. After all the hurtful things he had said and hateful things he had done, he still cared. I was going accomplish my goal because he would be at home tonight watching over me. *He wasn't going to get away with this. He wasn't going to leave me.*

"The whole bottle. One after one after one……" I let my voice drift off like the soft waves from an ocean that I played in my mind.

"Where are you?" Stan asked.

"The bathroom, I think."

"Can you make it upstairs to your mother's apartment?"

I did not like that question. "Please come home." I said in my most pathetic voice.

"I can't I'm almost out south, but I'm going to call your mother." Stan hung up the phone again. I was fucking haven't drunken water in a week lemonade yellow pissed.

A few minutes later Beyonce's voice was coming from my phone. I checked the screen hoping it was Stan calling me to say he had turned around and for me to hang on until he got there. It angered me to see my mother's picture with her name and phone number. So the son of a bitch did call her. I did not pick up. "Nobody fucking cares!" I screamed.

I started picking up all the tiny white pills on the floor. *I should take them all. Then they would be sorry when I was dead, especially Stan. Then again maybe not. He would just move the girl in who was calling at three o'clock in the morning. Styles would have a new mother. He probably wouldn't even remember me; he's only two years old. A dead mother is better than a crazy one. A bottle of Claritin won't kill me anyway. I think I would just have really clear sinus cavities.*

My poor baby. He had seen too much in his two years on this Earth. Hell he had seen too much in this one day. I watched my parents try to kill each other and turn right around to fuck each other with the same intensity. I would listen to them make their animalistic sounds which scared and confused me. I was never sure if they making love or war. *I'll never do that to my child*, I would think as I lay with a pillow over my face. I am a liar.

Styles watched as I stood in front of the doorway telling Stan I was not going to let him leave. Stan pushed me out of the bedroom door and I fell on my back. That was it. I just remember me grabbing any piece of his body that I could while glasses and chairs fell. "Mommy, please stop." Styles said it over and over but I had tunnel vision. I was on a mission Can't Let Stan Leave. I held on to Stan's leg like I was a dog in heat. He dragged me up the stairs and threw the mud. Stan kept punching me as he commanded, "Let go of my fucking leg Kristina."

"You are not leaving me like my father did!" I could taste rain water and blood. I caught glances of some of our neighbors' heads in windows. The heavy rain did not discourage others to come on their porches to watch the live show of the new, young couple at 1123. Stan hated to have 'scenes' in public. He was one of those people who needed to be the 'nice' guy. It was all about keeping up appearances. Sometimes I wanted to smack the shit out of him because he had to say hello to everyone on the street. Or when he knew someone when we went somewhere he had to hold a two hour conversation with them. He was a people pleaser, except when it came to Styles and me.

I, on the other hand, was like those old Sprite commercials. Remember the slogan image is nothing thirst is everything. I did not give a damn what you thought about me. Stan scooped me up in his arms like he was saving me and then took me back inside. As soon as it was just Styles, him, and me he dropped me on the carpeted basement floor. Styles screamed no.

"Look at how your father treats me." I replied to Styles. Styles saw me go get the gun and tell Stan he was not leaving.

Styles saw us wrestle for the gun that was directly pointed at him. If there had been any bullets in the gun, my son could have been another innocent child killed by gun violence in Chicago heading the ten o' clock news that night. Styles screamed for us to stop; but we didn't listen. I am ashamed to admit that hearing the police banging on our front door is what actually made us stop.

"Someone called the police. Open this door or we'll break it down." a voice said at our front door as they knocked so hard I thought the glass on the door would shatter. Stan dropped the gun and attempted to run to the front door. For once I had an advantage of being 5'2 to his 6'3; I slipped between his legs and made it to the door first. I knew that for the most part the story people heard first was the one they would believe. I opened the door to find two big, Irish descendent Chicago policemen at the door. Once could pass for Conan O' Brian on steroids with his freckles and red hair. I bet they were those types of cops whose father and his father before him were cops. I knew they would not be sympathetic to Stan or me because we did not come from their old country. Our fathers were not cops. In fact our fathers did not consider being a police officer an honorable profession. My father described them as "killers and thieves with badges."

"Miss, we got a call that there was a disturbance going on", the one without freckles said but his voice was not kind. His tone was very stern, threatening even. The way he called me miss he might as well had said nigger. His politeness was procedure, but he didn't want to help. Although Stan was quiet and Styles had stopped crying I could feel them both behind me. Even at two already Styles knew the procedure for a black man around police officers.

"I didn't call for you all. Everything is fine." I said not convincing them or myself. Their faces were red from a combination of the summer heat and the irritation of being bothered to do their jobs.

"Well someone called and for good reason", the cop without freckles said raising his voice. Conan was looking past me eyeing Stan like he had x-ray vision.

"Everything's fine", I repeated with sternness. Cop or not I did not like anyone raising their voice at me.

"What happened to your arm?" Conan asked pointing to my arm. I looked down to see a long gash on my arm. I honestly did not have a specific answer. I knew it was the cause of fighting with Stan, but I was stumped on how it got there. Dried up blood and mud was on the white tee I wore of Stan's that I had slept in the night before. My legs and arms were ashy from being dragged across the rug, then the concrete. I knew my hair was ruined from the rain and the tussling.

"I don't know", which wasn't a lie because I did not know exactly how I got the scar. The cops were not pleased with that answer. They both gave each other a look that let me know they thought I was one of those women with battered wife syndrome. They thought I was protecting Stan so he could beat my ass again. Reality was I did not want Stan to tell the cops what was going on because I could go to jail too. "If there is any trouble don't be scared to call us okay", was what the one without freckles said but I could tell from his tone he really didn't mean it. As soon as they left Stan was trying to follow behind them.

"I can't live like this." Niggers calling. Police and shit. Then you pulling guns. I'm leaving", Stan said as he started packing an overnight bag. *How can I pay the rent without him? What will I do? Why is he doing this?* I panicked. I started breathing hard and crying.

"Please don't leave", I said as I took a piece of clothing out of the bag as soon as Stan put it inside the bag. Stan grabbed my hands so I could not remove any more of his possessions. He stared me straight into my eyes. "I'm leaving."

He might as well have called me a bitch or whore. Those two words hurt me just as much. All I could see was red. I was desperate. He let me go and continued to pack. I ran to the bathroom. I went right to the medicine cabinet and popped off the top of the first bottle I saw. Stan was right behind me. "What are you doing?" he asked watching me open the bottle.

"I'm going to kill myself", I said as I began to pour pills into my hand. He knocked the bottle out of my hand. Tiny white pills exploded from the bottle all over the floor like confetti. Even after a good sweep months later I would still find a pill in little creases or crevices.

"You're fucking crazy", Stan said before leaving the bathroom. I could hear him turning on SpongeBob Square pants for Styles. Then I heard a smack. Stan kissing Styles on his cheek I assumed. Next I heard the front door close and keys locking the door. I slammed the door and locked it.

Now I was here where he had left me, sitting on the bathroom floor amongst the pills. I read the clear shower curtains with the black writing over and over again. It was the only item I had brought for the apartment that Stan liked. *Oh, not it's Monday. Clean behind your ears. Sing out loud. Who used all the hot water?* Rereading the quotes on the curtain seemed to calm my anger so that is what I did until they became jumbled together. *Oh, no who used all the Monday clean behind loud sing behind your ears?* I laughed out loud.

There was a knock at the door. "Go away", I said still laughing.

"Kris, its Ma open the door", her voice reminded me of the police who were aggravated.

Now I was angry. She was ruining the peace I had found. "Go away", I said harshly.

"You need to get out here. Your son has peed on himself and is hungry", my mother said. Her voice was unsympathetic. If I had heard some concern in her voice I would have come out. If I knew a hug and a *'There, there.'*

was on the other side of that door I would have come out. I was not coming out for *'I told you so'* and *'That's what you get'*. I had enough of those to last a lifetime. *Just once mother,* I thought *if you could be more loving.* This woman had more sympathy for the devil.

"I'm not his only parent. You have his father's number", I replied coolly.

"God damn it Kristina don't do this to me. Mark is upstairs. How many pills did you take?" *Do this to her? Leave it to my mother to make it all about her.*

"Sorry I interrupted your booty call. How's his wife by the way?"

"You crazy little bitch how many fucking pills did you take?"

"Who said I took some pills?"

"Stan said you took some pills."

"You always take his word! You believe everyone but me!" My cool tone became shrill and whiny like a child who couldn't get the toy they wanted in the store. Hearing myself I wanted to spank and hug myself all at once.

"Kristina, come out now!"

"No let me die here." I lowered my voice again.

"If you don't come out, I'm calling the police."

"Call them. They should know the way. They've already been here."

I could hear my mother walk away. I giggled to myself. I could not comprehend why I was enjoying torturing her emotionally. I pictured her having to tell Mark's fat, black naked ass that he better leave before the police got here because her crazy daughter was *at it* again. I was rolling on the floor laughing when I thought about what if the same two cops came. Wouldn't I just have ruined their day?

Why not ruin their day, Stan's day, and my mother's day. Fuck their days, my life had been ruined. I was rolling on the floor cracking up with laughter with Claritins stuck to my butt, back, legs, and arms. By this time I was laughing hysterically like I was in the audience of Def Comedy Jam. All of sudden my roars of laughter turned into violent tears. I started crying so violently my stomach and head hurt. After awhile I went numb as if I were in an emotional coma. My senses were revived by flashing lights I could see through the bathroom window and I could hear the alarming screams of a fire truck.

Somebody started banging on the door. "What's her name?" I heard an unfamiliar male voice ask.

"Kristina", I heard my mother say.

"Kristina, are you okay?" the unfamiliar voice asked.

"Who is that?" I asked suspiciously.

"Your mother called us, we're the firemen. Are you able to open the door?"

I couldn't believe my mother had actually called them. I couldn't believe that Stan had actually left me. Two plans foiled in one day.

"What are you going to do to me?" I asked. I could feel another panic attack coming on.

"We're here to help you Kristina, but we can't do that unless you open the door. I promise we won't hurt you." The fireman's voice was soothing like a mother kissing a scrape on her child before putting a bandage on it. I sat contemplating on should I or shouldn't I. I knew I could not live in the bathroom forever. I just wanted to be alone to recuperate now the whole Chicago Fire Department was in my tiny basement apartment.

"What's going to happen when I open the door?" I asked buying some time.

"We just want to take you to the hospital to make sure you are okay."

"I don't think I am okay. There's something wrong with me." I said as my voice started shaking. I was trying not to cry.

The fireman's soothing voice responded, "It's okay if you're not okay. Just come out so we can fix it."

Before I opened the door I checked my face on the mirror on the medicine cabinet. My face was pale and all my blemishes, like my acne scars and dark circles under my eyes, were visible without make up. My eyes were blood shot red. My hair wasn't as bad as I thought. Just a few misplaced hairs. I combed it and rubbed some Pink Moisturizer on the ends. Then I rubbed some Vaseline on my lips to give them some shine and then some on my eyelashes after I combed them to make them appear longer. I took a deep breath and opened the door.

There were about ten firemen in my apartment for little old me locked in the bathroom. Most of them were not impressed with my miraculous emergence and started heading back outside to their truck. My mother rolled her eyes. I could now see the soothing voice who had talked me through. He was handsome in a Christopher Soprano type of way. I felt ashamed to stand in front of him undone. I realized that I had not showered that day. Then I felt even more embarrassed to meet under the circumstances that I had to be coached out of a bathroom. They all knew I was crazy with bad skin. The fireman, who talked me out of the bathroom, had dark brown eyes that were just as gentle as his voice.

He introduced me to a woman and man that did not have on the same uniforms as the fireman. "These are the paramedics who are going to take you to the hospital", my fireman friend informed me. Then he turned to them and said, "Take care of her."

"Can I put on some pants?" I asked. Everyone stared at my thigh high boy shorts I wore to bed.

"Of course you can", my fireman friend told me making me feel relaxed. That feeling changed as I went to my walk in closet where my dresser was. Everyone was watching me as if they thought I was going to grab a weapon and kill myself. I wanted to take a hot shower and coordinate an outfit, but I grabbed some khaki Bermuda style shorts. I slipped out of my house shoes so I could slide into snakeskin flip flops to match the shorts. Also they gave the outfit a kick.

They made sure I couldn't escape. A paramedic was on both of my sides while the friendly fireman followed behind. "It's going to get better", he said as he gave me a pat on the back. *It certainly couldn't get any worse*, I thought. But it did.

It had stopped raining so all my neighbors were out trying to see why there were two fire trucks and an ambulance blocking traffic. I bet they thought Stan and I had killed one another. They were disappointed just like the firemen to see little old me walking to the ambulance. I looked away from their faces as they stared shamelessly into mine. Kids were running up to the truck after the paramedics put me in. *This is what it must feel like to be a celebrity,* I thought.

"She don't look sick to me", I heard one girl say. "Her and that boy was going at it earlier. She's small, but she was giving him some go. Thought he'd be the one in the ambulance", I heard someone else say. I could hear the neighborhood gossips having the nerve to come up and ask some of the firemen what happened.

"Women problems", one of the annoyed fireman responded. I was sitting in the back of the ambulance wishing I would have killed myself to save face from this mortification. Death before dishonor.

The paramedics were way too chipper than I could appreciate in the current situation. The man got up front and announced he would drive like we were on a road trip. The lady was short with bright, blond hair. She reminded me of one of the girls from Saturday Night Live, but I can't remember her name. Before she did anything she explained to me why and what she was doing.

"I'm putting this seat belt on you so you won't hurt yourself", she said before she buckled me in. I wanted to laugh at that statement because they still thought I had tried to kill myself. "Now, I'm going to take your blood pressure so we can see if it's at a normal level", she said before putting the Velcro around my arm. *There's nothing normal about me.* "Now I'm going to listen to your heart." *Do I still have one?* As she listened to my hard thumps she asked, "Was that little cutie yours?"

"Yes", I answered. I wonder could she hear my heart sink. What a horrible mother I was. Styles was bawling and reaching out for me when they helped me into the ambulance. My mother and a few firemen tried to comfort him but he held his hands out for me. I ignored him just like I did when he begged me to stop fighting with his father and when he asked to use the bathroom. *Styles is going to be as messed up in the head as me,* I thought. I started to cry.

"Oh honey don't cry. It's going to get better", the blond paramedic said as she rubbed my wrist.

"No, it's only going to get worse", I said. Stan was gone and Styles was going to grow up like me except in a boy's form.

The blond paramedic held my chin up and said. "You're too pretty to cry." The intellectual side of me that read about revolutionaries wanted to curse her out but the side that read Vogue wanted to hug and thank her.

West Suburban Hospital was only five minutes away but it seemed so much longer riding in the back of the ambulance. Every car moved out of the way for us. Strangers peeked in to get a look. I felt like some important dignitary or royalty from some foreign land. The blond paramedic held my hand and I asked did I need anything like a trustee servant. I shook my head no as I began to look out the window. I studied the streets that I drove down all the time.

All my life I had lived in the Austin Area. It was a section on the Westside of Chicago where the people kept their grass and weeds cut, but let their children run wild. I was a product of my environment. I had criticized Stan for keeping up appearances, but I really was no different. I was always working out, buying new outfits, putting weave in my hair, dying my hair, and wearing makeup. I never took the time out to deal with my past. While the outside was immaculate the insides were in disarray. I was the dilapidated house with a brand new paint job sinking in the ground.

We pulled up to the emergency room. Although I could walk I had to be transported in a wheelchair for legal reasons. "Safety rules", the blond paramedic explained. She wheeled me into the emergency room. Before she left to speak with hospital staff she whispered in my ear, "You're going to be okay and you give that cutie a kiss next time you see him."

Two

People in the waiting room were staring at me just like my neighbors. The question was in their glares and frowns, *what's wrong with her?* I know it really confused them when I was rushed off to see a doctor immediately while they were left sitting in the waiting room watching CNN spitting up blood in a plastic cup or doubling over in pain.

The nurse who wheeled me into the room was fat with a pretty face and smelled like fabric softener. She immediately started asking me questions and filling out a form when I answered. I knew she was strictly about business from her demeanor which made me like her for some reason. I had run across too many people who didn't take their jobs seriously.

"Are you allergic to any medications?" she asked.

"Not that I know of." I replied.

"How do you feel? Are you drowsy, dizzy, or sleepy?"

"For the circumstances I think I'm okay but I'm always tired. That's normal for me." I replied.

"What type of pills did you take?"

"None."

The cherub face nurse tilted her head to the side and said, "We can't help if you aren't going to be truthful with us? There's nothing to be embarrassed of." Honesty wasn't working so I lied.

"Only two Claritins."

She wrote something on my chart. I was not able to read if I had convinced her or not. She then took my blood pressure and had me stand on the scale to get weighed. The nurse told me the numbers as she copied them on my charts.

Now I want you to change into a gown. I'll leave the room on one condition," she stared me straight into my eyes to let me know this was serious. I nodded to let her know that I understood what she was about to say was like The Torah. "You can't do anything to harm yourself." I nodded again but I was thinking, *what was I going to do in this room? Give myself a splinter with a tongue depressor?*

"Okay?" she asked in a stern but trusting and caring way. It was the voice of how a mother should sound when she spoke to her child. It was just the voice I needed.

"Okay." I agreed.

As soon as the nurse left the room I felt cold and alone. I was in no rush to take my clothes off to put on a paper gown with the back out. I wanted to go home but there was no turning back now. I had convinced everyone I was crazy and now I had to convince them I was sane. Truth be told I did not know which category I fit into.

The room was all white and sterile. *This is what an insane asylum must feel like. Is that where they are going to put me next?* I could see Stan bringing Styles with his new girlfriend while I would be too drugged up to curse him and her out. I could see Styles asking, "Who is this? Can we go now? Daddy, you promised to take me to Chuck E. Cheese." I started crying as the scene played in my mind's theater.

I forced myself to take off my clothes and put on the gown that could be used as an oversized napkin. I sat on the table shivering and waiting. Dressed in a white gown and shaking just like a crazy person. The room was like a mini Antarctica. The waiting for what was going to happen next was making me antsy.

This felt too much like the clinic on Division with the Foot and Ankle sign as a disguise. I had three *procedures* done there. The constant waiting, the paper gowns, the questions of medical history, and the cold sterile rooms were the same at the clinic as it was at the emergency room. All three had been Stan's. I don't know if that is a fact to be proud of or humiliated by. Some pro-lifers who were not fooled by the sign would stand out front shoving pictures of babies that could be on a bag of diapers next to pictures of fetuses that resembled barbeque beef. "Look at what you're doing to your baby" they would scream. These so called Christians and do gooders were the worst torturers I've known. To show a woman *that* before she goes to do *that*, you have to be cruel.

The people who profited from the *procedure* were no better. Roe vs. Wade had gotten rid of the hanger methods that ruined and killed so many women before me, but big business had taken over. I could see the doctors' Jaguars and Mercedes locked away from the protestors as I had to fight my way through them to get inside. When you made it inside the receptionist gave you a clipboard with papers to fill out because that's what you want to do when you're battling the demons and angels inside of you.

There was paper that let you know that they were not responsible if some of the fetus was left inside of you. Then there was the form that you understood that an abortion could put you at a higher risk for uterus and ovarian cancer. Next there was the form that let you know that the scar tissue left from the surgery could make it difficult for you to get pregnant or carry a child full term. If you didn't change your mind; you signed your life away and handed over the $300. They were smart enough to get the money first. The receptionist let you know that from this point on you could change your mind but you couldn't get the money back. Then you signed to let them know you understood that. Now you could get on the assembly line.

Put on your paper robe, wait, next your ultrasound, take your number, and then wait some more until your number is called. "Number 8!" "Number 9! Hurry 9 we don't have all day!" I would jump like a ghost had tapped my shoulder each time my number was called.

What was a life changing event to me became an everyday task to the staff at the clinic. I recalled one time at the clinic as I lay waiting I could hear two women in colored scrubs talking in between calling numbers. The one in the turquoise scrubs that matched her eyes said, “It was gross. Seeing that little bastard all bloodied almost made me puke. Number 5!” An alarm went off in my head. *How could they be so insensitive.* I thought as I held my tummy still full with a fetus. I could see the pictures in the pamphlets that the protestors outside had given me of bloody, dead babies crying while the nurses chattered mindlessly.

“We had a time getting his arm through, it came off. Number 6!” the nurse continued on as hot, angry tears streamed down my face. I was about two seconds from getting up and grabbing that nurse by her neck until I heard her say, “After seeing that mouse trap I told Rick we’re moving. I don’t care how cheap the apartment is. I can’t live finding rodent carcasses around the house.” I wanted to laugh out loud when I realized how overly sensitive I had been or how idiotic the nurses’ water cooler chat had been.

Before you went to the *final frontier*, they had you wait in this room the size of a closet that they locked you in. They made it clear again that you could change your mind but the money was not refundable. “You wasted $300!” is what Stan would say. He wouldn’t ask if I was okay or could we handle another child. There was no turning back now.

You could hear *it* happening on the other side of the door. The sound is like the buzz saw in the scary movie when they are running from Jason. My instincts were to bang on the door and scream until they let me out. All three times I didn’t though. I took deep breaths and waited for my number to be called. I always paid extra to be put to sleep. I would wake up not sure what had happened with sore inner thighs. My friend Clarice once joked that maybe all the doctors had probably ran a train on me before they started the procedure.

Afterwards they would take you to a room full of beds with girls who had just had *it* done too. Some girls would come back like the living dead with drugs still in their veins or walking slow with solemn faces as if they were in a funeral procession. Some would scream like they had just awoken from a nightmare. I would lay in bed in the paper gown with the paper sheets over me as my teeth chattered.

Like this hospital room the walls, sheets, and gowns were white. Just like me all the women would tremble. Some hollering quietly, others loudly quiet like me, all of us in pain. All of us pondering the damage we had done to our bodies and minds with these abortions. We laid there thinking about the what ifs, the should haves, and could ofs. I had never been to the insane asylum yet but I was sure the waiting room at the Foot and Ankle clinic resembled it closely.

The nurse came in with a glass of what appeared to be charcoal and water mixed in a blender. She smiled tenderly at me as she said, "I'm going to need you to drink this for me."

"What is that for?" I asked.

"It helps get rid of the medicine in your system."

"For two Claritins?"

The nurse gave me that maternal voice again, "If you don't drink this we will have to pump your stomach by sticking a tube down your throat." I stared at the glass for a minute waiting to see if a cigarette was floating around in it.

"It looks like charcoal and ashes." I said trying to be sarcastic.

"It is." The nurse said being dead serious.

"Is this safe?" Which was a funny question coming from someone who had tried to kill herself, well at least the nurse thought so.

"I wouldn't give it to you if it wasn't. Now stop stalling or I'm having them come in with the tubes." I had irritated her.

I sighed before taking the glass. As I swallowed the nurse directed me not leave a drop or she would have them get the tubes. I took it in one gulp. I handed her an almost clean glass besides a few leftover particles of charcoal grains. It tasted how it looked. I felt like I licked an astray full of butts.

"Now was that so bad?" the nurse asked smiling. Why was she smiling I'm not sure. Either of pride because I chugged it or she took pleasure in my discomfort.

"Easy for you to say." I replied sticking my tongue out to see if it was black. I was so grateful that she handed me an apple juice.

"I have someone outside who wants to see you." The nurse said as she laid some warm cotton blankets over me. *Stan! He had heard I went to the hospital and was sorry. I knew he loved me.*

"Who?" I asked trying to contain my excitement.

"Your mother has been waiting outside." The nurse answered.

My heart sank and I turned on the other side to shield my face from her so she would not see my tears.

"I don't want to see her."

"It's your choice and I'll go tell her, but I know she's going to be so upset."

"No she won't. She doesn't care. She never has."

"I don't know how your mother has treated you in the past, but she cares now. It took me so long because I was out there comforting her. I'm a mother too and I couldn't imagine if one of my girls were in here. And then not to be able to see them…" the nurse stopped short. I didn't have to turn around to face her to know she was close to tears.

"You just don't understand…" Now I was close to tears. I couldn't finish my sentence because of the lump in my throat made it difficult to talk. When I got in trouble when I was younger and my mother wanted me to answer her I couldn't because of the lump. My mother thought I was being a smart ass so she would slap the belt against my skin and say "Answer me." This would only make me sob more making the lump in my throat bigger so I couldn't answer my mother which would make her hit me again. It was a vicious cycle.

The nurse rubbed my back as I wept. Her touch and scent was comforting. "There, there", she said, "You're just tired. Your mother told me all the stuff you've been through. You just need to be babied. We all do. Even my big ole' self needs a hug from my mama." The nurse tried to laugh hoping it would be contagious but I let the tears run down my cheek. I wondered how my mother could tell this nurse what I had been through when she did not know all that I had been through.

The nurse turned my chin so I was face to face with her. "Let me get your mama so she can give you the hug you need."

"She'll only yell at me and tell me how stupid I am." I replied.

"I promise she won't, but if she does I'll throw her out myself. Okay?"

I hesitated before agreeing with the nurse again, but I wanted to trust in someone so I finally said, "Okay."

Before the nurse left out she smiled and said, "I'll be back pretty girl."

As I lay in bed I wondered who all knew about me being in the hospital and who all cared. A few minutes my mother walked in with blood shot eyes. She had either been drinking, crying, or maybe both.

She ran to my side with crumbled tissues in her hand. "Is this my fault?" she asked before busting into tears. I answered by crying along with my mother. We hugged each other as we cried. Two drama queens at our best. My state wasn't my mother's entire fault but she was responsible for some of my trauma. I didn't have the heart to tell her. I was just glad she was here now. Two females with lab coats holding charts ended our soap opera moment.

The ladies excused themselves and then went on to introduced themselves. I didn't hear their names because I got caught in the rapture of my mother wiping my face with her used tissues. I assumed they were some type of therapists. One was skinny with mousy brown hair and thick black rimmed glasses. It was like someone had brought the cartoon character Thelma from Scooby Doo to life.

The other one had dark hair also but it was longer. She was taller and curvier than her partner. She reminded me of Catherine Zeta Jones without the glamour. Glasses did most of the talking while they both took notes. I felt like a chimpanzee being studied at the zoo. Glasses asked me to explain all the events that had led up to me being in the hospital.

I told them the whole truth and nothing but the truth, except for me not taking any medicine. I kept up my story of taking two tiny white pills.

"Why did you get so mad at your boyfriend for leaving?" glasses asked.

"My father would always leave when I was younger and I wasn't going to let Stan do it too. Their pens went wagging away after I answered.

"Your mother told us you had an altercation with your father a month ago. What happened?" Before I answered I glanced at my mother for a quick second. Not that he didn't deserve it but my mother wasted no time bashing my father's name.

"He didn't agree with me moving in with Stan, but I didn't feel that he could comment on Stan because he was a better man than him. I mean my father is a bum. At least Stan works. And my father didn't raise me so it irritated me for him to make judgment on me. I've been mad at him for a long time. So I just picked up a lawn chair and threw it at his ass."

They wrote at an alarming speed. "Maybe I have a problem with men." I smile. Zeta-Jones smirked but Glasses was stoned faced as she proceeded with her next question.

"Why did you take the pills?"

"I just wanted some rest and Claritin usually makes me drowsy." I was good at making shit up off the top of my head.

"So you didn't want to kill yourself?"

"I don't think I wanted to kill myself but I did want a nice, long sleep. But not an eternal one."

"Do you want to kill yourself now?"

Maybe if you keep asking these questions.

"No. But sometimes I don't want to exist. Sometimes I just want to disappear or be someone else but I don't want to die."

"Your mother told us about your full schedule", Glasses flipped through some papers. She began to read from the papers, "You have a two year old, go to school full time and work full time." Glasses looked up from the papers back to me, "Is that why you wanted some rest."

"Yes."

"Is there any other reasons why you wanted rest?" The way Glasses said rest made it clear it was a synonym for suicide.

"What do you mean?" I asked turning the table on her.

"Like any other traumatic experiences you may have experienced?"

I was quiet for a moment. I could feel three pairs of eyes piercing through me.

"I was molested in kindergarten and I was raped at fourteen." I didn't sound like myself. I had never said it out loud. It had just popped out.

"Oh my God!" my mother exclaimed before pleading to the women, "I didn't know about this."

"She didn't know about me getting molested, but I told her about the rape when she read my diary and found out I wasn't a virgin. I told her I was raped but she said I was a liar and a whore." I sounded like a robot. There were no feelings in my voice as a retold what happened when I was fourteen years old.

"Kristina, I don't remember that." My mother said horrified.

I turned to face her, "You were drunk."

"Have you ever had any therapy or counseling?" Glasses asked.

"I was trying to see a counselor but I couldn't fit it in to my schedule. Stan said it was the only way he would move in with me." The ladies both nodded.

"Is there anything else?" Glasses asked as her eyes darted between my mother and me. It was clear my mom was still in shock from the bomb I just dropped. I had lifted a ton of boulders of off my shoulders and placed them onto my mother's.

"I've been treated for having a chemical imbalance. Maybe that affects her too." My mother said. *Your chemical imbalance is anything in a wine bottle mother dear.*

Glasses sighed before speaking. She seemed to be annoyed with it all. "It sounds like your daughter's break down seems to be situational but we want to observe her overnight so we can be sure." Glasses went on but I tuned her out. All I could hear were the words 'breakdown' and 'observe'. I was one of *those* types of people now. The ones who everyone whispered about behind their backs and walked on tippy toes around them.

I had a great aunt on my father's side that had a nervous breakdown when I was a baby. Whatever decision she made was explained by that time in her life when she was ill. If she quit a job someone would comment, "Well you know she had that nervous breakdown." If she broke up with a boyfriend it was because she had that nervous breakdown. If my grandmother was telling a story in reference to one of her four sisters and someone would ask which one was she talking about she would reply, "The one who had the nervous breakdown."

Maybe they call it a nervous breakdown because whenever you are in a room full of people you are nervous because you are constantly wondering how many of them are breaking you down to just plain old crazy. Your are not a person anymore with feelings, talents, and situations. You are just a nervous breakdown. It did not matter that my aunt was the type of person you could tell you are a prostitute and she would not judge you. It did not matter that she made the best caramel cakes. I wondered when she died were they going to put the one that had the nervous breakdown on her tombstone. Were they going to put it on mine now? I did not think it was possible to have a breakdown at twenty three. I'm living proof for all the non-believers.

I was wheeled up to the fourth floor as my mother never let go of my hand. More eyes watched me in the halls and on the elevators trying to guess what was wrong with me. The room's perks were a small bathroom, a television, and a bed with a built in remote control. It was bare and beige. It was home to me because a wave of exhaustion came over my body. I happily got into bed and was dozing off as my mother kissed me goodnight. "I'll be back tomorrow. Don't worry about Styles. You get some rest." Those were the last words I heard before falling into a deep sleep.

I do not recall what I dreamed about but it wasn't pleasant because I sat straight up gasping for air like I was drowning. I panicked because I had forgotten where I was. The unfamiliar old lady sitting by my bed didn't help. *Was I still dreaming?* She was watching a black and white movie that she didn't take her eyes off of when she answered questions I never asked at least not out loud, "You're in the hospital. I have to stay in this room with you so you won't hurt yourself."

I was insulted. I felt like a newborn baby. I grabbed my cell phone on the table next to me. It was one thirty in the morning. I had no missed calls. I wondered what or who was Stan doing. Was Styles missing me? Where was he? Were they hugging him? Did my mother call my grandmothers and father? If so, what did they say? I wondered did my mother call my friends to tell them what happened. I just wanted to know did anyone care. None of them had called. Even with that intruder in my room I felt alone. I put the covers over my head and bawled as quietly as I could manage. The gray haired lady only came over to my bed to turn the volume up since the remote was connected to the bed.

I must have cried myself to sleep because when I awakened the sun was shining. I checked my cell phone again. It was nine thirty in the morning. There were still no missed calls. The old lady was gone and I was relieved. Another lady walked in with a tray of food.

"You finally woke up. I've been waiting to meet you. I'm Rosalie." Her voice was booming. It there were any particles of sleep left in me she destroyed them. She sat the tray down on the table next to my bed.

"I hope you're hungry. We got oatmeal, an apple, milk, and orange juice." She said in her stereo surround sound voice. I picked over the food. The oatmeal was watery and the apple was bruised. I decided I was not hungry.

"I'm not hungry." I replied turning my head away.

"Girl, at least eat the apple. You need something in your stomach." Rosalie insisted. I shook my head no.

"Alright picky eater.", she handed me a pen with a menu of choices, "Choose your lunch and dinner because you have to eat. I'll have the apple." Rosalie attacked the apple with her mouth. She chewed just as loudly as she spoke. I was hoping I wouldn't be here by dinnertime. I had the same nostalgic feeling for home when I spent a few days in the hospital when I gave birth to Styles.

I circled anything and left it on the table. I turned my head to the side to look out the window. Rosalie mumbled on even as she crunched on the apple. "These apples don't taste as good as the grocer by my house. Not juicy or sweet. I wonder is this a red delicious or a granny Smith. Some apples are only good for baking not eating. *I'm going to store that in my who gives a shit file.* I missed the gray haired lady already. At least she was quiet.

"You want to watch television? You got a remote built in the bed so you can change the channel you know?"

I only nodded yes to let her know I knew. I turned back to the window so she would get the hint that I did not want to watch television or talk.

"Well if you don't want to watch TV let me turn to the Price is Right."

Rosalie walked over to my bed to turn the channel. I could hear beeps from the wheel spinning as the audience squealed.

"Come on 20,000. No, no, no not that one. Shoot 5,000. Better than nothing I guess." Rosalie was entranced by the game. I wished she would shut up. I could tell she was one of those annoying people who talked through a movie. "No, don't go in there. I knew he was going to do that."

Rosalie had a hard face to look into. Her café au lait skin was covered with freckles and moles. She had a gap in between her teeth that was big enough that another tooth could fit in the space. She wore thick, big glasses that I suspected were older than me. Rosalie also had a turkey neck. As my grandmother would say 'when God closes a door he opens a window' because Rosalie had shiny, straight, black hair. She had a French braid that reached the middle of her back.

"A loaf a bread for a dollar, he ain't been to the grocery store in a while.", Rosalie commented on a player on TV estimation. *Would she shut the fuck up?* I wanted to yell that at Rosalie. I just wanted to be alone. I just wanted someone to call. I started crying again but this time I did not try to hide it. I don't think I could if I wanted to from Rosalie. She turned from the television.

"Are you ready to stop being ornery so we can talk?" She said as she pulled her chair up to my bed. I shook my head no as snot and tears ran down my face. Rosalie got up to get some tissues from the bathroom and handed them to me.

"Fine, then I'll talk. That's the one thing I'm good at. My husband says I'll be talking after they bury me." I was surprised to hear Rosalie had a husband. *Who could stand to wake up next to that moley face and loud mouth?* It was as if Rosalie was reading my mind because she went on, "I've been married to my husband for over thirty years and we got five children. All of them decent and levelheaded." I translated her last comment to mean that Rosalie thought I wasn't decent or levelheaded.

"My husband was and still is a fine man, looks and other wise. All my friends and his friends wondered what he saw in me. But you know what? I never did. I know I'm not the best looking woman but I have things that really matter. Honesty, hardworking and a strong faith in God."

As I continued to wipe my face with soggy tissues Rosalie went on, "You are a pretty girl but that will fade with time. So you got to have something on the inside or this world will crush you. Life is hard but you should never try to take your own self out. Life is a gift from God and honey you don't look no gift horse in the mouth."

Rosalie paused as she got me more tissues from the bathroom for me. She was quiet for a minute and just sat by my bedside. The only sounds were of me sniffling, blowing, and wiping my nose. It was no use in explaining to her I really didn't try to commit suicide. At that moment I realized that wanting people to think I tried was just as harmful as doing it for real, maybe even evil and sad.

Rosalie checked the watch on her wrist. "My shift is almost up." I wanted her to stay now. It was just nice to hear someone else fill up the uncomfortable quietness.

"Will I be by myself?" I asked.

"Naw, someone else will come in."

We sat quietly for awhile watching another game show until Rosalie asked me did I go to church.

"Sometimes." I said

"Promise me you'll start going now or at least you'll read the bible." Rosalie nicely demanded.

I promised Rosalie that I would but; if ten years of a Catholic school education hadn't brought me any closer or made me trust God I don't think church or the bible was going to be the cure. God was another man as far as I was concerned and they had brought me nothing but heartache.

"Let me leave you with some advice my mother told me and all five of my sisters that have never steered us wrong. Trust in no man just Jesus." Those were the last words Rosalie said to me before she left.

I was brought a lunch of a choke turkey sandwich, milk, apple juice, and mixed fruit. I drank the apple juice, took the sandwich apart, and rearranged the fruit with a spoon. Just as I was getting comfortable with being alone someone knocked on my door.

"Hey. How are you doing?" There was a Mexican Rosie O' Donnell with glasses with a short mullet standing at my door holding boxes and a big bag.

"Hi." I responded with no eagerness or pleasantries.

"I'm Hildita. Everyone calls me Hilly. My hips look like mini hills. Right?"

I was not calling a grown ass woman Hilly. She came to move the tray of food. Hildita or Hilly inspected the tray.

"You didn't eat a thing. Is that how you stay so skinny?" Hildita chuckled as she proceeded to eat half of the sandwich I hadn't destroyed. *Do they feed these people here?* She put a puzzle box on the table between us with her other hand before she sat down in the empty chair.

"Do you like puzzles?" before I could answer Hildita went on and on. She fit piece after piece telling me about her life story. I knew she was thirty five and lived alone except for her five cats. She was the only one out of her siblings who was unmarried and without children. Her parents told her she had brought shame to them. However Hildita seemed very satisfied with her old maid life of volunteering at a hospital, living with cats, putting together puzzles and being overweight.

She was a Saturday Night Live skit waiting to happen. Hildita's life sounded just as sad as mine. I wanted to make room for her in my hospital bed. I could see her slitting her wrists soon or maybe she was killing herself slowly with food overdoses. A heart attack or diabetes would sneak up on her soon like a trained black ninja assassin in the night. After polishing off my sandwich she began to nibble on some pork rinds she had in her big bag.

"Want some?" She asked letting pieces of rinds from her mouth splatter on my face. Pork rinds and chitterlings were two foods that I had vowed to never eat in my life no matter how hungry I got.

"No, thank you." I said wiping my face with intense disgust.

Hildita apologized. She treated me as I assumed she did when she was at home with her cats talking on and on. If she asked a question she answered it herself. I felt sorry for her and wondered how she could put on being so jolly when I could see her dying inside. I guess Hildita wasn't so different from me.

Every day I went to school and work with a smile on my face. I bet none of my co-workers or fellow students would ever guess I was spending Labor Day weekend in the hospital for attempted suicide. People were always telling me, "You got it together, Kristina. You work, you go to school, you take care of your son, and you do it all looking great." How wrong they were. Maybe my drama teacher Mrs. Marshall was right in suggesting that I pursue a career in acting. "I see big things in your future, kiddo."

There was a slight tap at the door. I stopped hoping for Stan anymore. I just hoped it was someone who cared. It was

Zeta-Jones from the night before. She smiled heartily and I tried to return the favor. “Can I see Miss Avant please?”

“Oh sure.” Hildita replied getting up. She knocked pork rinds and puzzle pieces on the floor. She was so awkward. Any other time I would have bust up with laughter but I felt sorry for her. In that fat shell I could see a piece of me wanting some acceptance and love. The more she tried to clean up the bigger a mess she made. I realized that Zeta-Jones was making Hildita nervous like she had a school boy crush. A light bulb turned on inside of my head. It all made sense now; no husband, no kids, mullet, and being raised by Mexican Nazi extreme Catholics. Hildita was a closeted lesbian.

Three

Zeta-Jones smiled sun rays at me before she sat in the chair next to the bed. She had a pad in her hands. "Remember me? Dr. Lombard." She asked. I was grateful she had told me her name again.

"Yes, where is your partner?" I asked her.

"Working with some other patients."

"I knew she didn't like me." I said in a matter of fact kind of way.

Dr. Lombard laughed slightly before she started on, "Actually I really wanted to speak with you. I have more experience with sexual victims. Is that okay?"

I nodded because I liked her bed side manner better anyway but I also took note that she never stated that Glasses did like me either.

"How has your stay been?" Dr. Lombard asked.

I wanted to complain about the food and the old lady who thought watching television was more important than me the patient but instead I said, "Okay." For the most part everyone else had been nice.

"You're probably wondering why I'm here. Right?" The doctor asked.

"I'm assuming to talk to me to see how crazy I am."

"I don't think you're crazy. Just traumatized.", she started, "That's why I wanted to know a little more about you. Have you ever discussed the specifics of your molestation and rape with anyone?"

I was a little peeved that the doctor was so interested in what a couple of guys had done to me in the past when I wanted to focus on what Stan was doing to me now. "No." I answered.

"I think that is why you are acting out because you've never really dealt with those terrible things that have happened to you. Talking to someone about them is the first step. Also I'm going to recommend that you meet with me at least once a week. If not me then another professional to help you get through this." Dr. Lombard said.

"I don't have time to catch my breath let alone meet to talk about my feelings once a week." I objected.

Instead of disagreeing Dr. Lombard asked me why was I so busy. "I'm a full time student at International Academy for starters." Before I continued on she asked me what I was studying.

"I'm getting my bachelors in merchandise management and I should graduate in December."

Dr. Lombard asked me what exactly everyone else asked me when I told them what my major was. "What is that exactly?"

"It's like business and fashion mixed together. My goal is to become a fashion stylist for magazines or celebrities but now I'm not so sure."

"Why not?" The doctor asked.

"The need for stylists in Chicago is not as big in LA or New York and I can't go to those cities with a baby. To be honest the only reason I went to this school and chose the major was because one night when I was up all night throwing up from being pregnant the commercial came on asking do you like fashion. I do; so I enrolled. I wanted to prove everyone wrong who was saying I would never graduate from college with a baby."

"So what are you going to do in December?" Dr. Lombard asked me giving me an intense gaze.

I sighed before answering. "Keep working as a waitress and maybe concentrate on my writing. My creative writing teacher and my arts in humanities teacher both asked me why I was wasting my time with fashion when I had a raw talent for writing.

"Do you like writing?"

"It's hard to say. It doesn't come as easy to me as fashion." I started, "But even as a little girl I could remember making up stories and writing them down. But I would never finish them."

Dr. Lombard shifted in the chair without taking her dark coffee colored eyes off of me. She seemed to be intensely interested in what I had to say. I had to admit that I was enjoying talking about myself.

"You don't come off as the waitress type to me. Do you like it?" Dr. Lombard asked.

"You're absolutely right. I'm not the waitress type, but I'm responsible for half of the rent and I like to shop. Stan got me the job. He works in a law firm downstairs from the club I work at. I hate serving people who spend on banquets what I make in a year. I'm just a servant. No one sees my talent or style or beauty because my hair is all back and I have on this ugly black tux."

I went on, "All they care about is can I get them some coffee and do I know the recipe for a certain dish. It's hard to watch people experience the best times of their lives when you are so miserable. It's the longest I've ever worked a job though. The pay is nice and my co-workers are some of the nicest and hardest working people I've ever known. Plus I've seen Oprah Winfrey. Her boyfriend Steadman is on our Board of Trustees and he's extremely polite. I also served Jesse Jackson who is tall and very charming in person. The club is always full of movers and shakers who run this city."

"Wow, that's quite an impressive list." The doctor exclaimed.

"Yeah, but I get depressed meeting those people. Bringing them a drink reminds me of how much of a nothing I really am. My biggest fear is to end up working there for years just so I can support Styles and me."

The doctor paused before asking me another question. I guess she was soaking in all of what I said. "Do you like being a mother?" It was time for me to pause.

"I love Styles but I don't like being a mother. I'll be the first to admit that I'm selfish and you can't be like that when you're a mother because the child comes first. He's always there needing something whether it's a hug or a bag, or something. Sometimes I feel like I'm emotionally broke and there's nothing there for Styles. Stan always has that option to just up and leave but Styles is attached to me. Sometimes he feels like a growing tumor."

"Why did you have Styles?"

"I had gotten pregnant before by Stan and got an abortion without any question. He was so hurt but I felt we were too young and I was the only one working at the time. Stan told me love was enough to raise a baby. So a few months later when I got pregnant again and Stan had a decent job with the law firm, I thought it was my destiny to have a baby with him."

"Seems like what people say seem to have determined your choices for some important decisions in your life. Would you agree?"

I turned to stare out of the window. I had always thought of myself as strong and independent woman who didn't give a fuck what anyone thought of me. That had all been a lie. The doctor was right. The only reason I went to school is because the majority was saying I couldn't do it with a baby. The only reason I had kept Styles was because of a statement Stan had made. The most important reason I had gotten back together with Stan and moved in with him was to prove all the naysayers wrong especially my very own father. I was letting others' thoughts and words rule my actions.

"I always thought I was an independent thinking rebel.", I paused, "I guess not."

"It's normal behavior to a certain extent to let loved ones' opinions affect your actions. Tell me about Stan."

"Ironically I was already involved with another guy named Stan when I met this Stan. The other Stan was not paying any attention to me so when I started working with Stan number two it was easy to fall for him. We would stay on the phone for hours and he would take a bus way across town just to see me when my boyfriend who stayed a mile away with a car wouldn't."

"I felt guilty cheating but Stan number two was going away to college soon so I was going to write him off as a summer fling. It didn't happen that way because we still remained close after he left. Every time he came home from downstate he made an effort to see me. We talked on the phone for hours every night. When we ran out of things to tell each other we listened to each other breath. When we got tired we held the phone up to our ear while we slept."

I smiled recalling the *good* times. "Subconsciously I did everything in my power to make him not like me. I would get drunk in front of his friends and embarrass him by running around naked. I told him how I had stripped for one summer after graduating high school. He knew about the many men I had been with. He was the only person I confessed to about the molestation and the rape."

I began to tear up, "Any other guy would have dumped me on the spot but he stayed and still put me on a pedestal even when his people didn't. He wiped my tears after I cried, after sex or whenever. My best friend was like why don't you dump the other Stan and stick with Stan number two. So I've been with him on and off ever since."

Dr. Lombard nodded like she understood perfectly. "He sounds like a good guy. Is he still like that?"

"No just the opposite. Every since the first abortion there's been some type of wall between us. I try to break if down but my hands just end up bloody."

"Has there been violence other than yesterday?"

"Yes. I'm ashamed to say that I've sometimes started it. Sometimes he just ignores me and I want him to pay attention to me anyway possible whether it's fighting or fucking me. Lately those have been the only two options. That's pretty sick isn't it?" I asked the doctor.

No it's not for someone who grew up in an abusive home or was the victim of sexual abuse. Was that the case for you?"

"Yeah, my parents fought. I can remember them being violent right around the time I was being molested in kindergarten. Up until kindergarten my childhood was bliss. I was the happiest girl in the world." I chuckled picturing me with long, twisted ponytails and ruffled dresses I insisted on wearing. My mother would affectionately call me her little Mexican.

"It's interesting that you associate the first memories of your parents' violence with being molested. Why do you think that is?"

I really tried to think back to those times. It was supposed to be happy times. Playing with Barbies and dressing up in old clothes sort of times. Putting on plays for grandmothers' times. My parents were engaged and had moved in with one another. I was starting school and getting my very own room. My father brought me a brass bed with dancing ballerinas doing classic dance positions on the sheets. I would imitate the first and second positions on my sheets when I was alone.

It was 1985. My mother was a secretary in an downtown office and my father was an operator at AT&T. He had nicknamed himself 'the smooth operator' after the Sade song that was popular at the time. It was the eighties so my parents did everything big. They went into debt spending money on clothes, the apartment, and me.

Every pay day my father had a bag from the mall and my mother had a bag from Michigan Avenue. We were the picture perfect family in designer coordinated outfits with an apartment to match. My mother showed off her decoration and cooking skills by inviting people over on the weekends. Fridays and Saturdays were party nights. If I was not spending the night over one of my grandmothers I would want to stay up late to be a part of the interesting party scene in our home.

My father's friends would put me their shoulders and give me dollars while my mother's friends would tell me how cute I was. I was given the nickname She-rah because it was my favorite cartoon character and my father had bought me all of the action figures from the show. The saddest time of those parties is when I had to lay in thc dark while Cameo played on my father's new stereo system. I fell asleep with the memory of everyone having a good time without poor, little, old me.

Every weekend the party was at our house and I was put to bed at eight o' clock. One night I decided to get up because I heard voices I didn't recognize and I wanted to see who they were. I crept around the large apartment unnoticed because it was so crowded. People were drinking or smoking or both. Very few danced to Talking Heads playing on the stereo system. Mostly my parents' Caucasian friends. My father had went to college with whites and fell in love with some of their music. I loved to sit with while I studied the Police, Queen, Led Zeppelin, and Pink Floyd album covers. That was our thing. His friend from the old neighborhood didn't understand why my father listened to that cracker music but I got it.

People partying in out apartment were too preoccupied to pay attention to a five year old in pink pajamas. I didn't recognize any of the people and my stomach began to hurt. It was wall to wall strangers. I wanted my mother and father. I turned the knob to their bedroom door. I could hear a lady telling a man. "She shouldn't be going in there." But it was too late because before she could get the complete sentence out I had opened the door.

I found my father and three other men sitting on the bed around a mirror with white powder in neat lines. Another habit my father had picked up from the white boys at college. My father was snorting it with a dollar bill. The men got quiet. The only one I recognized, Joe, tapped my father's shoulder so he could look up. "Get out of here!"

It was the only time my father yelled at me. He might as well branded me on the bottom with hot coals because it would have hurt just as much. I ran to my room, jumped in the bed, and pulled the covers over my head. I never wanted to come out of that cave of sheets. I would never speak to my father again. My feelings were so hurt. My mind was confused. I kept thinking, *What was the big deal about snorting baby powder off of a mirror and why did it make my daddy so mean?*

From my memory it seems that it all went downhill from that moment. My room was next door to my parents so I heard the arguments about missing money from my father's check because of all the days he was calling in sick. Then he lost his job altogether. So instead of the arguments being about my father's shortened checks they were about unpaid bills and growing debts. The shopping bags and weekend parties disappeared. My mother started working more hours to cover the slack.

Although there were no more extravagant parties at our house strange men came over when I was with my father after school. They would go to the den to play loud music and close the door while I watched Jem and the Holograms, Thunder Cats, and then She-Rah. Now I knew better than to open the door. I assumed they were snorting baby powder off the mirror again. One day when I was getting dressed for school I put some baby powder up my nose to see what would happen and all I did was cough.

One day when I was coloring in the kitchen I mentioned about the men who came over to my mother because I didn't think it was a secret. I assumed she was aware because they came over all the time. She drilled me like a detective would a murder suspect. Had I been left in the room alone with these me? How did they look? What did they do when they were here? After that I was sent to a babysitter's after school until my mother got home from work.

The babysitter was one of my kindergarten classmate's mother. My mother had expressed the need for a babysitter when we saw them at the neighborhood laundromat. The lady had volunteered since she was home all day with her own children because she worked nights. I wasn't so keen on the idea because I disliked my classmatc. Hcr namc was Tiffany. I teased her like all the other kids in out kindergarten class. She had a cleft lip which made her talk funny and she was deaf in her left ear. Being different was not celebrated or embraced in the kindergarten class at Byford elementary. Tiffany might as well have been a space alien to me. I never thought our worlds would collide.

The first day I was at their house Tiffany along with her fat older sister made me pay for all the taunting for Tiffany's birth defects and her sister's juvenile obesity they both received at school. One would pull my ponytails while the other would hit me in my stomach. The fat sister would sit on me while Tiffany would torture me with pinching and punching. They got away with it because their mother would sleep like she was in a coma once she picked us up from school.

She would warn us before she dozed off watching General Hospital, "Which ever one of you little mutherfuckers wakes me up I'm beating your ass." My eyes watered at the thought of getting a spanking. That mean lady's yelling was upsetting enough for me. It didn't matter that I obeyed by being quiet as a church mouse not wanting the wrath of God to come down over me because Tiffany and her sister would make noises then blame it on me.

As a matter of fact I got blamed for everything in that household. "Who in the fuck got jelly on the goddamn table?"

The mother would yell. Tiffany and her sister would sing in unison, "Kristina did." The mother would exclaim, "Which one of y'all bastards was playing with water in the bathroom?" Even though Tiffany and her sister's tee shirts were drenched in water I got blamed.

"Listen you little bitch. I don't know what your stuck up ass mama let you do at her house but you gon't sit your ass down at mine." Is what their mother would tell me when I was wrongly accused. It's funny how people try to be hateful or ignore you they don't realize they are still giving you lessons to be better in life. What I learned from that evil, cruel lady is to never be phony. It was amazing how she spoke when my mother was around. I was such a pretty well behaved girl when my mother picked me up. As soon as my mother was out of sight I became a son of a bitch. I didn't understand it then and I don't understand it now: how some people can hate me so strongly.

As we would walk home to our apartment I would ask my mother why I couldn't stay with my father. "He can't watch you and look for a job." She would reply but neither one of us believed that. Whenever we got home in the evening my father was in the same spot in the bed where we had left him that morning.

"But they nasty. It's always crumbs and paper on their kitchen table. And it stinks in that house. It's always dark in that house like a haunted house. And their peanut butter is watery. And all of them hate me. They all pick on me." My mother didn't respond to not one of my complaints she only corrected my grammar. "They *are* nasty."

The arguments between my parents turned into fights. My mother had broken my father's finger by throwing a leather and steel dining room chair at him that he tried to catch before it hit his face. My father gave my mother a black eye. She dropped his stereo equipment on the floor so it would never play again. Even though my father could not listen to the expensive sound system again, he never had the heart to throw it out. My father put my mother's three hundred dollar hot pink suede boots in the toilet and then urinated on them. The tit for tat seemed never ending.

There is nothing more disturbing for a five year old to leave the house in order, including a newly decorated Christmas tree, then to come home to find it in shambles. Broken glass from thrown dishes or ornaments covered the hard wood floors. Every piece of furniture was out of place or turned over. I imagined this was how the Gestapo left the houses when searching for hidden Jews. Seeing the Christmas tree laying on the ground as if it had been murdered traumatized me. I dropped to my knees and screamed, "What have you done to my Christmas tree?" I got no answers. Even though I was loud my parents couldn't hear me because they were already passionately making love in the bedroom. During that period in my life I felt that no one was listening to me. I stopped pleading for my parents to stop fighting. I stopped begging not to go to the babysitter. I took Tiffany and sister's double team tortures and tattling. At night I would pray for the situation to change. And it did.

Tiffany's thirteen year old uncle moved in. Now he would be in charge while their mother slept. God heard my prayers. Not only did the uncle stop Tiffany and her whale of a sister from teasing me, but he would also turn the tables on them. He would mimic the way Tiffany talked as he formed his lips to look like her disfigured ones until she would cry. He would give the sister wedgies and hold treats up in the air to make her jump for it like a fat, trained seal. I would laugh out loud as her sweat mixed with tears while she heavily breathed.

When they threatened to tell he would remind them that waking up their mother would get a belt across their tails and she would believe him because he was the oldest. Being kids life had already taught us that whoever was the oldest is usually the one adults were going to believe. I told my mother time and time again how Tiffany's mother slept all day and said 'bad words' when we woke her up but Tiffany's mother had over twenty years over me. So my mother; even though she had carried me in her womb for nine months, known me all my life, and raised me; took the word of an adult she had only known for a few weeks.

At first this uncle was fun but anything was better compared to his unconscious troll of an older sister. She would ask us what we wanted to do and we would yell out, "Hide and go seek!" "Farmer in the dell!" "House!" or "Watch cartoons!" I don't know why Tiffany and her sister even yelled out suggestions because he would only let us do what I wanted to do. He would play along with us which was entertaining at first. Then it became weird.

We would lay on the edge of the uncle's bed watching cartoons. Instead of going to the side of the bed to lay down he would climb over me so his crotch was in my face. It felt uncomfortable because I knew that his private parts had no business in my face. I would tell him to stop. He would smile saying he was only trying to get in the bed. "Well use another side then." I would instruct him.

When we would play the farmer in the dell he always took me as his wife. His hugs lasted too long. If it was hide and go seek he would change the rules to whoever he caught would have to give him a kiss. Tiffany and her sister wouldn't try to hide. They were so obvious behind drapes and under the dining room table giggling. I wondered why they wanted to be found and kissed by their uncle. It didn't matter because the uncle would ignore them and concentrate on searching for me. I hid in closets and inside the tub behind the shower curtains. The uncle would always find me so he could put his tongue in my mouth. I would push him away, "I don't want to play anymore. You don't play right."

When I did that he would let his nieces have their way with me. They were even more meaner like a pit bull that had been caged up and gotten his first taste of blood. The nieces hated me more because I had become the object of the uncle's affections. Life was miserable again. I started letting the uncle kiss me for protection. The kissing never got easier. I always gagged because I could taste whatever he had eaten that day. He was my friend again. He would give me candy and make Tiffany cry because she had to play with the Ken doll while I played with the only three Barbie dolls the girls hadn't destroyed.

One day he took it a step farther. We all wanted to play house. He was the father, I was the mother, and Tiffany and her sister were the children. I pretended to cook while Tiffany's sister complained that she should be the mother because she was the oldest out of us girls. "It's night. Time for bed." The uncle said. He made his nieces lay on the floor at the bottom of his bed and I had to lay next to him. We all pretended to sleep by snoring loudly like they did on the Bugs Bunny cartoons with our eyes closed. All of us girls giggled because we sounded so silly.

My eyes were still closed when I felt his rough lips against mine. The uncle then slipped his thick tongue into my mouth like he always did. I could taste sour cream and onion flavored potato chips on his breath. When I felt him unzipping my pink corduroys I sat up. "Stop." I commanded.

"This is what mommies and daddies do. So if you don't want to do it then you can be a kid and let someone else be the mother." The uncle said. I didn't want to be a kid. I didn't want to do like mommies and daddies either. I heard my parents in the room next to me and it sounded like it hurt. "I promise it will feel good." He said as he gently pushed me back down on his twin bed.

He kept exploring my mouth with his tongue as he felt around my Hello Kitty underwear with his fingers. I cried, "You said it wouldn't hurt." I could feel his finger trying to penetrate me. He didn't apologize. The uncle got up to pull down his jeans and underwear while he gazed intensely at me. I have forgotten the features of his face now just like some of the nasty details of what he has done to me. Yet I see him in every man I have dealt with since then. When I rewind my mind to these specific memories his face is a dark circle with an insert here sign but I could pick his penis out of a line up. It favored a long, thin turd to me. I was absolutely horrified. *What was he going to do with that?* I had never seen a male's private parts before.

He pulled my underwear and pants down to my knees before his thirteen year old body got on top of my five year old body. He rubbed our naked privacies together. Even though I couldn't see them I knew Tiffany and her sister were watching from the bottom of the bed. All of sudden the uncle started moaning. I could feel wet stuff on me. I thought I had peed on myself.

"Wait right here." He said as he put on his pants. He came back with a towel to wipe me off. "If y'all tell how we play house then I won't play with y'all again." The uncle said addressing not just me but his nieces also. When I got home I threw those Hello Kitty panties behind the radiator in my bedroom.

When I started peeing on myself I started hiding those underwear behind the radiator in my room. Every day before I went to school I would throw tantrums to stay home. On rare occasions it would work and I would get to stay home with my father. To lay next to my father in bed and watch cartoons felt wrong. If my father or one of my uncles would try to hug me I fought with them to stop. Their affections seemed to have ulterior motives. Children's games that I used to enjoy before the uncle had turned into foreplay.

Eventually the uncle stopped using the 'house' game. He would just make all us girls *touch* and *do stuff* to each other while he watched. He called it 'juicing'. He would *touch* his nieces too but I seemed to be his favorite. It seemed to me that

Tiffany and her sister enjoyed their uncle's sexual games. They were extremely jealous when he made them take a nap so he could lay on top of me to leave his DNA all over me. He always wanted me to touch him down there. I would cry hoping that would discourage him. My tears made him want it even more.

When we watched cartoons he would sit me on his lap and made me roll my hips like I was playing with a hula hoop. I would always do what he told me thinking this will be the end. Then he will be satisfied and then he will stop, but he never stopped. When I did one nasty act he thought of another even more disgusting one for me to perform. *It's never going to end.*

I wanted to tell but I was too humiliated. I couldn't even attempt to let the words form from my mouth to tell my parents how the uncle had stolen my innocence. They were too wrapped up in their own drama to notice how I had went from a precocious, bubbly child to a dark, depressing five year old. My father rarely came home and my mother was always tired from working or worrying. Sometimes I got the feeling my parents knew what was going on and that is why they avoided me because they were ashamed of me. Some way they had figured out the dirty secrets the uncle made me do. Instead of facing me my father stayed out in the streets and my mother worked long hours.

I had gotten to the point that I couldn't take the uncle anymore. My stomach would bubble when I thought of him. Every time an adult looked at me I knew they saw a girl with stained panties. They could see all the sexual acts the uncle had made me perform. I woke up, ate, played, and slept with guilt. I just wanted out. I became obsessed with suicide. Sometimes that seemed the only way out without confessing all of the sins I committed.

It was the weekend and I spent the night over my grandmother's. It was the happiest I had been in awhile. It was the one place the uncle had not tainted in my life. My grandmother's house was my place to escape. She let me watch cartons and eat all the chocolate candy I wanted. I was learning the days of the week so when Sunday came I knew that my Monday thru Friday hell was not too far away. My body began to tremble and I exploded with a volcano of tears until I vomited all over the kitchen floor.

After my grandmother cleaned up my waste she held me and frantically asked me what was wrong. "I can't tell you because I'll get in trouble." I said as fast as I could because the lump in my throat hurt when I spoke. My grandmother promised me I wouldn't. I sobbed some more as she rocked and hugged me. "It's going to be okay." My grandmother said it over and over in my ear like a chant. She turned me around by my shoulders to face her, "I can't help you if you won't tell me. No matter what it is I will always love you."

After I finally calmed down I told my grandmother every sordid detail the uncle had done to his nieces and me. I told her details that my mind was kind enough to block with time. Since that Sunday I never told anyone the specifics again. I just told Stan I was molested at five and I cried as he held me. "What type of person does that to a child?" I asked through my tears. He did not have an answer.

I vaguely recall the exact details of what happened after that Sunday but I never went back to the babysitter's or back to Byford Elementary where I was classmates with Tiffany. My grandmother switched her shift at her job so she could stay home with me in the day time. I don't remember if my grandmother told me not to tell anyone else or not because I never spoke of it again until I met Stan.

I forgot all about the uncle until one night I was having sex with Stan. He poked a spot inside of me that seemed to unleash all of those ugly memories. I screamed for him to get up and began crying uncontrollably. I could tell by Stan's faced he was scared and confused. "Did I hurt you?" He asked.

"No, not you someone else." He held me and I told him. He was very loving and caring. "I never told anyone that." I told him as I drifted off to sleep in his arms. That was not completely true because my grandmother knew. What I won't forget is the look on my grandmother's face. It was a mixture of mortification, shock, and knowing all in one if you can picture that. It was never mentioned between us again. I always wondered if my grandmother told my mother what happened because my mother never discussed it with me.

I always had an inkling my mother knew. When she would give me a bath at night she would lecture me on the different body parts and how I should tell if someone touched me in a bad way. It was too little too late. I don't know if this was a figment of my imagination but my mother and grandmother couldn't seem to look me straight in the eyes anymore. The very evil that my mother was trying to protect me from my father's new found mirror sniffing friends had found me anyway. She had failed me. And my father had also.

My father wouldn't pick me up and swing me in the air any more. He didn't make fart sounds on my cheeks anymore and call me kissee face. Sometimes I would think that he stayed out for days not to see me. My father avoided me like I was a contagious disease when I needed him more than ever.

I never saw Tiffany, her fat sister, or their uncle again. However those feeling of shame and anger have never left me. When Stan or any man touches me sexually I'm that five year old girl again: scared and unwilling. That seems to arouse some men even more when I tell them no. When they finish my tears are mixed with their semen on the bed sheets. What makes me confused and nauseous is that the more abusive and humiliating the sex is, it seems like I enjoy it more.

Four

Before I could answer Dr. Lombard's question of why I associated my parent's fighting with being molested there was a knock on the door before it swung open. It was my mother and my grandmother wearing big smiles for me.

"Hello Dr. Lombard." My mother said, "Should we come back?" Dr. Lombard stood up and said, "Oh no. I can come back later. I think Kristina is sick of looking at me anyway." The doctor gave my hand a squeeze before leaving the room with my mother. My mother said she would be back and ask did I want something. I shook my head no. My grandmother sat towards the bottom of the bed.

She held my hand. Although her lips formed a smile her eyes glistened from tears forming in her eyes. I had only seen her a few day before but since then she had aged decades. There was a line for each time I had upset her and piece of hanging skin for each favor I had asked her for. She had five children and eight grandchildren but I always knew I had a special place in her heart, mind, and soul. I was the fifth daughter in our family's special female lineage. First there was my great-great grandmother Octavia which we lovingly called Big Ma. Big Ma only had one child which was a girl she named Laura Bell. Laura Bell, my great grandmother, went on to have five children but only one girl which she named Rebecca. Rebecca insisted that everyone, even her children and grandchildren, call her Beck. Beck, my grandmother, repeated history. She had five children but only one girl which was my mother Melinda Gale. Then Gale, because everyone called my mother by her middle name, had me Kristina Joi.

"It's going to be alright, baby." It was the same phrase she said when I told her about the uncle. Instead of comforting me the words of supposed encouragement made me angry. Her words were just another one of those lies adults tell to put a bandage on a leak. The water builds up over years and the truth bursts through.

"No it won't. It hasn't been all right in all these years and it never will." I turned my head towards the window. It appeared that I was staring outside but it was all blank. My grandmother's visit was reminding me of the uncle and how I would never forget what he did to me. Even when I got to be sixty five years old like her those dark memories would be in my mind's attic.

My grandmother turned my chin so I could see every crease and crevice in her Georgia clay colored complexion. "You got to pray Kris. I've been praying for you."

"Don't you come in here talking about God and Jesus." I said in a low growl like a dog giving warning that it was about to attack. I didn't sound like myself but like some possessed evil being. "I've been going to Catholic school all my life and praying since I could talk and God has not answered one of my prayers yet. That's all black women know how to do is to fucking pray."

"In slavery they taught us to pray to their God to make us weak. If our kids are getting molested or on drugs. We pray. When our families are destroyed. We pray. When we are broke and need some fucking money. Dying of aids, then pray."

My low growl had turned into a high pitch shrill. "We need to stop praying and take action. I'm tired of dropping on my knees and being subservient waiting on some imaginary, all powerful man to save me."

My grandmother gave me a glare that played back a memory in my mind that I had forgotten. Since my grandmother quit her job to stay home with me she decided to babysit other children for money. There were two boys around my age. Their names had been erased from my mind like the uncle's face. My grandmother let us play on the sun porch. One hot summer day we played every game twice and was extremely bored.

"Let's play with my Barbies." I suggested. The boys never wanted to do that. "Let's play G.I Joe." One of them proposed. I reminded them that I had played it with them once already and it was boring. No one wanted to color. It reminded us of school too much. We sat and thought. Two wires got crossed in my little messed up head.

"Let's play house." I said.

"That's a girls' game." One of them said.

"I know how to play house so boys like it."

That glare that my grandmother gave me in the hospital room was the exact one she gave me when she caught me doing to the two little boys what the uncle had done to me. Shades of anger, shame, and alarm were in my grandmother's face just as it was that summer day.

My grandma Beck got up to walk to the other side of the room. She turned her back to me. I could hear her sobbing and quietly praying. I had never known my grandmother to cry. I felt like the dirt on the bottom of a shoe for making her upset but I was so angry. I was so angry that I could see only lava red. Could I be possessed? Maybe I needed a priest and some holy water instead of a psychiatrist. My grandmother's whispers were growing louder. She was saying the Lord's prayer. It was the first group of words I had learned to memorize. I started crying again with my grandmother. "Why didn't you tell anyone about what the uncle did to me?"

My grandmother turned around quickly, "What uncle?" She asked.

"The uncle at the babysitter's house when I was in kindergarten. I only told you and you didn't tell anyone else. Why?"

Beck only stared at me confused. Maybe she had forgotten but how can you forget your five year old granddaughter painting you images of sexual fantasies instead of princess fairies. Then I thought to myself that I had only remembered a lot of images of the past today. The brain is like a cheating man sometimes; it will make you forget all the hurtful events you know happened. *Yes, she had forgotten to block out all of those terrible memories.*

"Tell someone for what?" My grandmother started in a low voice, "You don't talk about those types of things. I got you out of there and you were okay."

Her words stung me like a bumblebee. "In case you haven't noticed I'm in a hospital room because I faked trying to kill myself. I'm far from being okay." I slightly chuckled at my grandmother's delusion. I was surprised by my ability to still laugh.

"Kristina, you will be okay. It's just what happens when you're a woman. You just have to ask God for some strength." My grandmother went on. I was in utter shock.

"I didn't know that being violated was just as natural as getting your period. I missed that lesson." I replied sarcastically.

My grandmother had turned her back to me again and she faced the wall again. "Your mother was going through so much with your father. I couldn't burden her with that." We were both silent for awhile.

"I know how it feels to be a mother and find out what happened to your child." My grandmother started, "It's your job to protect your children so when that happens you feel like a failure. You are angry and helpless all at once. You just want it to go away. I couldn't put your mother through that. She's been through enough. I love her too much." There was silence.

I kept thinking about my mother, the only mother I knew. She had been the only mother I had ever had but as a child I sometimes I wished for another mother like my friends had. There always seemed to be a fire lit inside of her that had gotten out of control. As a child I thought it was my father, but when they finally separated when I was in eighth grade, it seemed like she still putting out on those fires unsuccessfully. My mother would use liquor to make her internal fires grow. I got burned by her so many times. Sometimes I hated her when she yelled ugly words to my brother and me. Other times I felt sorry for her when she would cry uncontrollably and unable to explain why she was crying. It all made sense to me now.

"So it happened to Ma?"

My grandmother turned to face me and her head nodded yes.

"How old was she?"

"Eight." My grandmother began to sob again.

"What happened when you found out?"

My grandmother walked over to the chair next to my bed and plopped down in it like she had carried twenty grocery bags up twenty flights of stairs.

"No one wanted a scandal. He was kept away from your mother. I was told she would be fine because she was young." My grandmother had a faraway look about her, "She would be fine with prayer." She went in her pocket of her jean shirt for her cigarette box to take one out but she stopped in mid action. I am guessing she recalled that she was in a hospital where you couldn't smoke.

"You know how Big Ma was taken advantage of when she was twelve and gotten pregnant with my mama. She had survived through prayer. When it happened to me I survived with prayer."

"It happened to you too?" I asked in amazement. My grandmother nodded yes again. "It's happened to a lot of women." *It's just what happens when you're a woman,* my grandmother's statement played over in my head.

"I've never told anyone." My grandmother studied my face as she paused. I guess she was considering if she could trust me with her secret.

My grandmother continued, "I was walking to my car after having a few drinks a neighborhood lounge. Usually I would have one of my brothers or one of their friends walk me to my car but everyone was on their own thing and I was ready to go. I was parked right across the street so I didn't think anything could happen."

"I remember opening my car door, then darkness. I woke up with my head hurting and a light skin guy with big, pink lips and freckles that covered his face on top of me." My grandmother stopped and got up to walk over to the window. She stared out of the window as she started back telling me her story. It was as if she was watching it happen all over again.

"I will never forget that face. That shit stained freckled face. He was on top of me breathing hard and pumping." My grandmother gagged like she was going to throw up and placed her hand over her mouth.

"When I realized what that bastard was doing I started screaming, kicking, and fighting." I imagined my fragile, tiny ninety pound grandmother trying to fight off some huge monster.

"It was no use because he had me in the alley behind the lounge. No one could hear over the loud music. Finally, it was over. Something must have scared him because he got up frantically, hit me in my face, and took off running." My grandmother stopped again to cover her mouth with her hand as tears fell on her chest. She went on.

"At first I was so angry. I got my pocket knife out and decided to chase that nigger myself but I thought about how he had socked me from behind. With what I don't know. Could have been a gun. Then I thought about what he did to me. I couldn't face him again."

"I decided to go back in the lounge to tell my three brothers. I knew they could and would want to beat his ass. Men had honor back then. They protected their women back in my day. I started to walk back to the lounge but I couldn't move my feet. Shame came all over me. I couldn't even imagine forming the words in my mouth to tell my brothers what that stranger had done to me. I ran to my car and drove home."

"I never told anyone. I could hear people blaming me. They would have said that I should've had someone walk me to my car or that I shouldn't have even been at a lounge in a mini skirt. But at home with my husband and children. I could hear all the criticizing."

"I kept the secret but I nearly went crazy. Every time I saw a light skin man with freckles I lost it. I stopped going out and lost my job from taking off too many days at work. I just couldn't risk seeing that face of that man again. But every night in my dreams that face popped up. It was in every thought that I had. I stopped sleeping with your grandfather because when he touched me a certain way it reminded me of that face of that man. I prayed and prayed and prayed. It's all I could do."

No wonder I was so fucked up in the head. I was fighting five generations of pain. My mother had been molested, my grandmother and great-great grandmother had been survivors of rape, and my great grandmother was a child conceived out of rape.

I wanted to be mad at the women who had come before me for not telling their stories to warn the next generation. There was no cause and effect explanations. They only gave orders. Don't wear revealing clothes. Don't hang out in the streets. Don't get pregnant.

If they had talked to me about what had happened to them then maybe I wouldn't be repeating their history. I wanted to blame my grandmother for her hush, be still and let God mentality but I couldn't. I got up and hugged her. I had some understanding now about me and the women who had all raised me. It was amazing how all these women appeared so domineering and opinionated yet all had been violated. Maybe that is what made them so loud on other issues because they were silently dying on the inside with secrets. I understood how important it was to talk about my issues so it wouldn't happen to my son or future daughter.

I let my grandmother out of my embrace once my mother walked in. My grandmother excused herself to go get some coffee which would include a smoke break with her Marlboro lights. She put on a pretend smile so my mother would not notice her tear stained face. I got back in bed and my mother sat in the chair next to me. She handed me three Snickers. My mother knew I felt about chocolate the way her and my grandmother felt about cigarettes. I could smell smoke mixed in with her Dolce and Gabbana perfume I brought her for Christmas. I realized how hungry I was and inhaled two of the candy bars without stopping to chew or breath.

"The doctor said she'll release you later on tonight if you feel comfortable. Are you ready to come home?" My mother asked with hope.

Part of me wanted to stay in this white room forever but realistically I knew I had to go home. "I can go home." I said while using my tongue to get a nut lodged in my back tooth.

"The doctor suggested that you rest this week. You can stay upstairs in my apartment." My mother suggested rubbing my hair.

I pulled my head away from her gentle caress. "I can't miss school or work.", I began, "This week is my finals and the rent will be due."

"If you tell everyone the situation I'm sure they'll understand." My mother replied.

"Why so everyone in my life can think I'm crazy? I will be well enough to go in tomorrow. How is Styles?"

My mother sighed before answering to let me know she disapproved of my decision. “Fine. I left him with your brother. Your grandmother is going to take him for a week.” I didn’t argue about that because I had no doubts about handling school and work but I wasn’t ready to see Styles. The image of him crying and holding hands out for me drained me.

My mother went on, “I went downstairs to let Stan know what was going on. He was down there with that little short ass boy he hangs with. Both of them too drunk or high to care.”

The thought of Stan’s short ass friend Brandon sleeping in my apartment and using the towels I had bought infuriated me. I guess Stan was having too much fun to call me.

“Did your grandmother Bobbie or father call you?” My mother asked. I shook my head no and looked down.

“I told them what happened”, my mother went on, and “You see your grandmother and me are the only ones here. I don’t know what my mother was trying to accomplish with her comment but it made me sink lower in my emotional quicksand. I turned to look out the window. It was a nice, sunny day. The kind of day that I would take Style to the park or ride around in a car with my best friends Clarice and Turiya. Instead I was in a hospital while life went on without me.

“I want to ask you something?” The serious tone in my mother’s voice made me turn away from the window to face her. My mother’s eyes were tearing up. By this time I was tired of crying and watching the others around me do the same.

My mother took a deep breath before she asked, “Was it a relative who did *that* to you?”

“No.” I answered immediately.

“Oh thank God.” My mother sighed this time with relief.

There were no follow up questions. She did not inquire with a who, what, when, where, or why. I wanted to ask her some questions but I didn't. I had suspected after the conversation with my grandmother Beck that a relative had scarred my mother. From my mother's question she thought the same relative was a repeat offender.

I had so many questions. Who was the relative who had done this? Was he still around all the new grandchildren and great- grandchildren. Was he still alive? Did my mother have to look him in the face every holiday? Is that why she had spent most of her childhood and mine swimming to the bottom of E&J? Now she had switched to wine. I guess alcohol had been her weapon of choice to numb the pain. I used heavy artillery because my weapons was sex, shopping, and alcohol.

Memories I had forgotten were playing against the white hospital walls from my minds projector. A few years after my brother was born my mother was like a robot. She would just stare at me like I had spoken Latin when I asked for a kiss or a hug. I don't remember her crying even after my father would hit her. There were no laughs. My mother was programmed to feed and bathe us. The alcohol had worked well for my mother, maybe too well. There was no life in that body. The alcohol in her not just numbed her from the pain of her life but the love that comes with living. My mother was emotionally the living dead.

We just sat in silence in that white room. If my life is ever turned into a movie and the background music for this scene of me sitting with my mother in silence in a white hospital room should be The Beatles 'Eleanor Rigby'. I just hear that chorus playing over and over like the memories of my childhood, *I look at all the lonely people.* Who were more lonelier that us in that white hospital room.

My grandmother came in and she sat quietly with us too. Some women pass down recipes or heirlooms; we had passed down pain. The silence had gotten too loud for me. For the first time ever in my life I wanted my mother and grandmother to talk. Usually their voices would irritate me. They would loudly criticize me and talk over one another's sentences that they would become one big force of nature. It was impossible to get a word in with these two around to defend myself. Their cackling didn't do much for my self esteem but they made me a worthy opponent for any verbal battle. To compete with them I had to have a loud, commanding voice and I hit below the belt. I had to with my mother and grandmother in the room. I always felt sure of myself until I was in the room with both or either one of them.

"You're going to wear that?", "You look better with your hair back.", "I guess girls nowadays don't wear panty girdles.", or one of them would say "The only women who wore blond streaks in my day were prostitutes." I wanted my mother or grandmother to break the unbearable silence even if it was with an insult.

I broke the silence, "How many people know I'm in here?

"It's nothing to be ashamed of.", My mother started off. I wanted to remind her when she was placed in a mental hospital on Mother's Day weekend when I was fifteen years old. My grandmother told me not to tell anyone. Only grandmother and me knew not even my little brother was told where our mother was on Mother's Day. *More secrets,* I thought.

"How many?" I asked again.

"I just told your grandmother, your father, your Uncle Kirk and Aunt Elaine, and your Uncle Phil and Aunt Gail." My mother responded nonchalantly.

"All of them." My grandmother, the professional secret keeper, blurted out.

"Not enough time to alert the media?" I asked sarcastically.

"It's nothing to be ashamed of." My mother said again. I think it was directed at my grandmother instead of me because my mother stared intensely at her while my grandmother rubbed my hand. It was official. I was going to be the crazy one. Stan was always telling everyone I was crazy. Here I was in a hospital bed proving him right. I could see his family and my very own tiptoeing around me like I was a time bomb ready to explode.

My grandmother expressed how she needed to get back to her house to start cooking dinner. Her and my mother kissed me on the cheek just as they were bringing my dinner in. "I'll be back to get you." My mother promised after she asked me what she should bring me. I told her to grab a white slip dress, my white sandals with a cork heel, and some lip gloss. For the first time I realized I had not showered in two days. I decided to do that after I ate.

Dinner was some undetectable meat covered in gravy with neon green peas and lumpy mashed potatoes. I covered the food back up and opened the last Snicker candy bar that was left. After the food attendant left I noted it was the first time I had been left alone since I got to the hospital. I supposed if they thought I was well enough to go home I could be left by myself. It could be a test or someone was just late to sit with me. A familiar silhouette with braids rushed passed my door then came back.

"Kristina." The girl said a bit surprised.

I instantly recognized the voice and the face.

"Hi, Sheena." I said embarrassed, "What are you doing here?"

"I came to bring my cousin something." She gestured with a nod of her head to the flowers with a little balloon in it, "She did some stupid shit to get in here."

I could tell Sheena regretted her comment as soon as it came out of her mouth. She looked me over realizing that I was laying in that hospital bed on that fourth floor ward because I had done some stupid shit too.

"Oh." I said because what else can you say.

"Are you okay?" Sheena asked. Her voice sounded concerned and nosy all at once.

"No, but I will be. I'm just tired."

Sheena tried to lighten the air and make up for her past statement, "Couldn't afford a vacation, huh?"

"Not that type of tired. Just emotionally tired. I've been dealing with a lot of things on my mind for years."

Sheena nodded sympathetically even though I knew she had no idea what I was talking about. She told me to take care of myself before she headed towards her cousin's room. I wanted to cry again but no tears would come out. I was all cried out like that Lisa Lisa and Cult Jam song.

Sheena grew up with me. Her sister was not only my beautician but the neighborhood gossip. Everyone in the neighborhood was going to give me those *she's crazy* looks too. When I walked down the street they were going to cross the street to the other side. *Out of all the people to see! Damn!*

I had always admired Sheena. She was the first feminist I knew. She would do whatever the boys did and never let them intimidate her. Everyone was always telling her to put on a dress so the boys would like her. I would get mad and hurt for Sheena when they would whisper that she was a dyke. Sheena wouldn't change for anyone. She was who she was. In fact she proved the naysayers wrong when she got pregnant at fourteen years old. Tasheena Shade wasn't gay and without a skirt the boys still liked her as much as she liked them.

Sheena didn't hide in the house or go down south either with her pregnancy. She wore her round belly under her athletic jerseys like a badge of honor while I wouldn't come outside because of a few pimples on my face. Again it was just her this is me and who I am attitude. One time I had a big, oily, juicy ready to bust bump on my nose. The only reason I was outside is because my mother threatened me to go to the corner store on Augusta to get her some cigarettes. I ran into Sheena who lived across the street from the corner store. She must have felt my insecurity because she told me, "Be glad it's a big bump instead of a big belly." Sheena rubbed her gut full of human. I always looked up to Sheena and wished I had her strength.

Why do some women get that strength and others don't? When adults in the neighborhood shook their heads and whispered behind Sheena's back she ignored them and rubbed her belly proudly. Whereas, when I get judged it sends me to a mental meltdown. Sheena was dealing with adult issues at fourteen standing straight and proud. Here I was fully grown at twenty three laying on my side.

Sheena was one of those success stories that parents could brag about. She had gotten married, gotten the dependable government job, brought the house, and had two cars in the garage. When anyone asked my mother or grandmothers about me all they could say was. "She's going to be okay." or "Well, you know Kris." Dr. Lombard could not have come in at a better time.

Five

"Ready to go home?" Dr. Lombard asked before closing the door.

"I have to.", I started, "I'm scheduled to work tomorrow and I'm taking finals all this week at school."

A concerned frown appeared on Dr. Lombard's face. "I wish you would rest," she sighed, "But it is your decision."

"School and work are the only times I feel worth something. Those are the only times I am happy. It's the only time I don't hurt." I paused waiting for a lump in my throat and water in my eyes but neither came. Like that old Lisa Lisa song I was all cried out. I went on, "Besides I don't want to be laying in my mother's apartment wondering what is going on in mine."

"What do you think is going to happen with Stan and you?"

I paused and stared out the window again as if the answer was outside. "I don't know." I said not really to Dr. Lombard but more to myself. I turned to the end of my bed where she stood and looked directly to her brown eyes. "It's obvious he doesn't care about me."

"Why would you say that?" Dr. Lombard was physically asking me the questions. But I felt like it was some bigger, inner being using her to make me finally think of the answers to these questions that needed answering for so long; but I fought and refused to.

"He hasn't called or visited me to see how I'm doing. He's been going on partying like I don't exist."

"You didn't get a chance to tell me about the rape. Did you want to discuss that?"

I noticed that the doctor wasn't writing on her pad anymore.

"Yes we can." I replied. I looked down at my hands that I was rubbing furiously together as if I was trying to start a fire. Although I relived the rape whenever a man touched me or spoke to me a certain way, I never told anyone the details of what happened. Not my mother, not my friends, not Stanley, not my grandmother, and not even my God.

"I was fourteen and my mother had finally left my father for good. She promised me that she wasn't going back. We moved into a raggedy apartment around the corner from the flea market on Division. I hate Salsa music to this day because on Saturdays and Sundays that was my alarm clock at 6 a.m."

"My mother was working full time at the airlines throwing bags on planes. We barely saw her. When she was home in the daytime my brother and I were at school. When we got home, her shift was starting; and by the time she got home, we were sleep."

"It became my responsibility to take care of my brother and the apartment. I was bored and lonely. Talking to your friends on the phone and watching TV can't take up a whole day. Because of my mother's schedule and her needing me to watch my brother, I hardly got to hang out with my friends. But one day I did. I went to the arcade in the Brickyard mall with some girls from my high school. It was the place for all the teenagers to be."

"That's where I met Rae. I instantly liked him because he had green eyes. I had never seen a black boy with real green eyes like emeralds."

"Oh but how he fooled and charmed me. He paid so much attention to me. I was so hungry for it! Both of my parents had starved me for it. They had made me an easy prey. He brought me junk food and gave me emotional food with kisses and hugs and compliments." I stopped to smile because I remembered the joy I felt at that exact moment.

"He even won me a teddy bear. The girls at school were so jealous. I think that's the first time I ever felt that feeling of someone wanting what I had or wishing to be me. I had always been the one dreaming to be someone else or somewhere else."

"Rae told me he played football and was a senior at Jones Commercial High School. So I'm thinking smart and athletic. I had hit the high school lottery. Rae called me every day and didn't hesitate to tell me how pretty I was. I thought Rae would be the perfect boyfriend."

"A week later the Gods answered my prayers because Rae asked me to be his girlfriend and I was honored to say yes. I was already picking my dress to wear to his prom. Once Rae found out the hours my mother worked he was begging to come over. I was scared I would get in trouble but I was so alone and he was my boyfriend. He explained to me that talking on the phone wasn't enough for a senior. So I finally agreed to let him visit me one Saturday when my mother left for work."

"I wasn't too naïve. I knew he would want to kiss and I wanted to too, but I had explained on plenty of our phone conversations that I was a virgin. Although I considered myself a rebel my Catholic school upbringing did influence me. I did believe in saving yourself for marriage. I thought Rae understood that because unlike most boys I had come into contact with he didn't try to change my view, which is probably why I liked him more."

"I waited for my mother to leave. Then I fed my brother and made him take a nap, then I put together the cutest outfit before I let Rae come by. As soon as he sat on the couch her was all over me." I paused again for a minute. I remembered at first how I felt happy because I wanted all this affection this man was giving to me. It was something I never experienced before. Having one being's undivided attention. In moments my joy turned to fear.

"I liked the attention, just like I did with the uncle who molested me. I kept thing 'Wow a cute senior who plays football and drives a car likes me. He kissed me on the lips and sucked my neck but when I felt his fingers under my skirt I stopped him. My stomach had that queasy feeling like with the uncle. He stopped but got an attitude. I remember sitting there wondering why kissing couldn't be enough for men."

"Rae showed another side of himself. He asked me could he use my phone to call a friend. I heard him telling his friend how I was scary and how his friend was right about him wasting his time with a freshman. When Rae got off the phone he turned on the television and ignored me. It was the uncle all over again when I didn't give in to his advances or my father after he got on drugs. I hated to be ignored. I tried asking him questions to spark a conversation but he acted as if nothing existed outside of that basketball game on the television. I stopped trying to talk to Rae and just sat next to him on the couch like a dummy. I swallowed hard and blinked constantly so he wouldn't see me cry."

"After a few minutes Rae turned off the television. I stood to let him out. I assumed he wanted to leave, but he walked to my bedroom instead which was off of the living room. He walked around and studied my room before he sat on my bed. I was thanking God that I had put my collection of Barbie dolls that I occasionally played with in my closet out of sight. I stood by the door until Rae grabbed me onto his lap and started kissing me. It reminded me of how they kissed in those black and white movies. It was the most romance I had ever had."

"After awhile of kissing he threw me on my back. I thought it to be a little rough, but he still kissed me passionately. He lifted my shirt and bra to lick my breasts. Even though it was dark because it was winter and the sun had already gone down I knew my face was bright red. No boy had ever kissed or seen my breasts before. Then I could feel his hands under my skirt again pulling down my underwear. I was scared to say something. I didn't want to make him mad anymore. I wanted him to keep kissing me, to keep paying attention to me. It was the closest I had felt to being loved in awhile."

"Stan uses that same trick when I tell him I don't want sex. As a matter of fact every man I've ever told no to for sex had used that trick." I snickered like an evil villain in a movie who had just figured out an evil plan to destroy the hero.

"I felt that God, my parents, and every nun who had taught me were watching. I told Rae to get up, but he kept grinding so hard I thought he was going to rub my hair off down there. I kept telling him to get up and stop but he wouldn't. I could feel him trying to stick *it* inside of me and then I started yelling no. I tried to push him off of me so I could get up. He smacked me in my face and then pinned down my wrists over my head with one of his arms while his legs held mine down." I couldn't help it but my voice was getting louder and louder. I felt like I was reliving it again. I wasn't in the hospital room but back in that tiny bedroom on Thomas Street by Kolmar Avenue.

"With his one free hand he stabbed my insides. I yelled no. It hurt like hell: my wrists, legs, and vagina. I didn't start crying until he broke me." I put my head down I didn't want to see the doctor or for her to see me. Shame was pulsating through the room. My voice was small again muffled against the white pillows.

"When I was little we'd sing songs as we jumped rope about getting your cherry busted. I could actually hear it. Like opening a cork screw off of a champagne bottle. I cried because there was no turning back now, there would be no saving it until marriage. Rae had taken something that I could never get back. As the tears rolled from my eyes I could see those green eyes. Those same eyes that I thought were so cute reminded me of snakes. He even began to look like an evil hybrid of a reptile and human. He wasn't cute anymore. I just wanted him to hurry up and finish so he could leave. Rae left all of himself all over me just like the uncle did. I wanted to throw up until I throw all of my insides up and didn't exist anymore."

"He did the typical guy move after sex and asked for a towel. They tell you how good you smell and how good you look but right after sex they try to disinfect every trace of your scent off of them and avoid your face as they leave in a rush."

"I didn't move from the bed to get Rae a towel. I was crying hysterically. That son of a bitch had the nerve to tell me to stop crying. He told me I should be glad it happened because if it hadn't have been him it would have been someone else who wouldn't have been so patient. That's when I started hitting and kicking him. He found my rage hilarious and my small fists of fury did nothing to his muscular quarterback physique. So I picked up a chair to my desk and hit him across the chest. I told him to get out. I was a little scared that he would kick my bony ass but he had already defiled me so what did that matter. Luckily after calling me insane he just left."

"I didn't tell anyone what happened. I just told my two best friends that I had lost my virginity so they would think I was grown up. I was always trying to prove something to them since I was the youngest and the one with the broken home. I even went to a dance at Weber High School for boys the same night. I meant my next boyfriend Sugie there. He was a freshman and on the basketball team, not football."

I went on talking even though she knew about all the dirty details of the rape. It was like I was in a trance. I could see Dr. Lombard's physical shell but I feel she is someone else. A spiritual being who knows what I am going to tell her before I say it. For the first time I am comfortable with this spirit and I want to tell it everything even though it already knows. I need to know it and hear it from my own mouth.

"He was sweet and polite. My mother liked him too, so two weeks later I gave him some sex instead of waiting for him to take it. He told me he loved me and bought me whatever he could with his allowance. I let him get on top of me whenever he wanted. One time even though it hurt I let him fuck me until I bled. I had gotten really good at concentrating on one object in the room as I lay under Sugie and the pain went away."

"Sugie began to bore me so I gave it to Money next because he seemed way more exciting because he was out of high school and had a nice car. Then there was Desi. I wouldn't say I gave it to him, but I didn't fight him off like I tried and failed with Rae." I turned away from the pillow to study the doctor. Although she didn't move or speak I felt her or something encouraging me to go on.

"It was my mother's off day and I didn't want to be in the house with her when she was drunk so I would just go walking around the neighborhood. Desi pulled up in a nice car and asked me if he could take me out to lunch. I got in the car with him because he was cute. He told me that he had to go home and change first because he had gotten finished playing ball. I thought it was exciting that he had his own place with two male roommates. He was a real grown up in my eyes."

"The apartment was nice too. As I sat on Desi's waterbed as he showered I thought his apartment would be a nice escape on my mother's off days. Desi came in the bedroom wet and naked. Although I was more experienced than my kindergarten days a dick still scared me shitless. Desi came in making small talk like being naked was nothing. He was asking me about school, what type of music I liked and how many boyfriends had I had."

"Desi continued the small talk as he pulled my panties off and slid himself right inside of me. I didn't want to do it but I got scared. I remembered his roommates in the other room. Then I kept thinking of a saying my mother had told a friend after a fight with my father: anything in your house can be used as a weapon. He pumped my insides full of himself while he asked me twenty one questions and I laid there answering them. With Desi's DNA all over me I lay in shock. As soon as it was over he didn't ask another question or speak another word to me. He put on his clothes and dropped me off on the corner where he had found me without lunch. My feelings were so very hurt, but looking back it could have been worse. He could have killed me, let his roommates run a train on me or anything…" I had to stop because it was the first time I realized how close I had flirted with death and yet I was still alive. Crazy and damaged but nevertheless alive.

"What slowed me down was I got sick a couple of weeks before I started my sophomore year. My lower stomach was hurting go bad I couldn't walk. My mother rushed me to the emergency room here at West Suburban. My doctor was cute and I was in utter horror that he was to give me my first pap smear. The doctor told us that I had a combination of gonorrhea and a urinary tract infection. My mother didn't even know I was having sex. I stopped having sex for awhile. I was too self conscious and even though the medication had cleared up the disease I felt dirty. My mother and I could have been guests on the Maury show: My teenage daughter is a slut with an STD." I uncomfortably chuckled at my own joke and turned towards the window.

I was wishing I hadn't said all that stuff. Now I knew she was judging me, scorning me, laughing at me. When she went home to her perfect home in Oak Park or River Forest with her successful husband and perfect well adjusted 2.5 kids, I would be the entertaining conversation piece as they ate their well balanced meals with their equally perfect friends on their patio.

'Let me tell you about this patient who came in this weekend', I could just imagine Dr. Lombard telling her husband and friends as she sipped her glass of wine, ' This girl is a Lifetime movie waiting to be made. She's been molested and raped. It's her own fault. A true slut if I ever saw one. Do you know she had the nerve to be shocked that she caught an STD? I don't need to tell you that she also another baby out of wedlock for our tax dollars to support. She aborted the other three thank God. She wasn't even successful at killing herself. A classic case.'

I thought to myself that I had not admitted the abortions to Dr. Lombard but I put it on my medical history when filling out the paperwork and I knew Dr. Lombard had access to my records.

Dr. Lombard spoke finally in reality and not in my fantasy. "Why didn't you go to the police or tell anyone else about Rae or Desi?" She asked in her inquisitive white women educated but caring voice. The higher being's presence I felt before was gone.

I didn't turn away from the window to face her, "Because they would all blame me. I wasn't supposed to have anybody in the house or get in the car with strangers. So I got what I deserved." I flicked through my brain like you do for songs on an IPod.

"I tried to tell my mother but she called me a liar, whore, slut, and everything else but a child of God. If your own mother believes that then why would someone else believe otherwise?"

"Have you seen or heard from Rae since?" This wasn't Dr. Lombard but the presence using her again because the presence knew I had seen Rae again. The presence was trying to remind me that it wasn't my fault.

"Yes.", I said in a matter of fact kind of way, "Well I didn't see him the first time. I guess you can say I heard about him and found out he was a liar. What a shocker right?" I could see the cars going up and down Austin Boulevard. It had turned out to be a beautiful day as I told all the horrible events that had taken place in my life.

"After my mother left my father for good I would go on the old block of Monitor to visit with friends I grew up with and my grandmother still lived over there. One of my friends had a cousin who was visiting with her this particular day I had come around. I was amazed that the cousin was seventeen like us with two kids. I kept asking her questions in reference to being a young mother and having kids because on the inside I was thinking I could've have been her. Instead of a curable STD it could have been a baby or HIV."

"From the girl's conversation I could tell she was simple minded. She kept talking about her boyfriend, the father of her children: Rae. She went on and on how he had cheated on her with other girls in their home. I was really half listening to the girl because I was thinking what an idiot she was. She continued on saying how he had a thing for young girls. He would go to high schools after school or where he young high school girls were. He would lie about being a senior football player at Jones but the reality was he was thirty years old. That's how he had got her but by the time she had found out the truth she was three months pregnant with their now three year old daughter."

"That's when something in my brain clicked when I looked at the one year old boy the girl held in her lap and her daughter by her side whining for another cookie. Both of the children had those same wine candy apple green colored eyes that I will never forget. I did the math. Rae was really twenty six when he pulled that shit on me."

"My first instinct was to tell the girl, but for what? He had done so much to her already and she still wanted to be with him. I left abruptly and started walking home without saying good bye to anyone. I had to get away from those whining kids and their screaming eyes. As I walked home I plotted revenge on Rae but when I got home I thought about how many young girls he had destroyed like me. Then I thought how can a young girl like me on her own destroy the devil. Getting out of high school was enough."

"A few months later I saw him in the mall with the girl and the kids. She was pregnant again. Our eyes met but she looked down. I don't know if she was ashamed to be pregnant again or because she had realized I was one of his victims. Rae looked at me too and like his girlfriend he recognized me too. He smiled like the Cheshire cat in Alice in Wonderland. I gave him a cold look that could have turned him to salt. I wanted to kill him but it wasn't going to give me back what he had taken from me. I've learned to live with or maybe I haven't learned to live with what has happened. I don't know." I took a breath.

"I used to feel that the pain was inside of me and now I think I'm inside of it. I was always too scared to try drugs thanks to my father, but drinking, shopping, sex, and crying was easy and accessible. But nothing makes the pain go away forever only for seconds."

I sighed gazing out the window at the perfect day made for perfect people. Everyone in their cars off to barbeques to taste new, happy moments while I was in a stale, white hospital room still regurgitating old, miserable moments. I was numb. *Is this how my mother felt when I tried to kiss her and she turned her head away? What hurtful memories had her in a time capsule?*

I was in time warp too. I was not twenty three. I was still a traumatized five year old who wanted her parents to make it better. My body had matured but inside I was still a fourteen years old who had given up on her parents and now wanted a prince charming to rescue her. I had thought Stanley would be that prince; but he had disappointed me like everyone else I had trusted with my hopes, dreams, and love.

For some reason I remembered another childhood memory. I could see a fuzzy image of my father's mother and me in her Buick. She would take me wherever I wanted to go and buy me whatever I wanted but there was no negotiation on her smoking or changing her radio station. So I would eagerly look out the window until we got to our destination inhaling More cigarettes in the green pack while the easy listening station played in the background. It seemed like that station only played five songs. I don't know the name of this song or who sung it but it starts off something like this, "*I can see clearly now the rain is gone. I can see all the obstacles in my way……It's gonna be a bright, bright sunny shiny day.*" That is exactly how I felt at that moment.

I realized that my issue was not just with Stan but every man who I had come in contact with. When I tried to fight or hurt Stan I really wasn't doing it to him. He represented all the men who I had put my trust in only to have them hurt me: my farther, *the uncle*, and Rae. Looking back I had never trusted or depended on myself but I never thought I was strong enough which made me an easy prey for the predators.

"Am I strong enough?" I asked out loud to myself as I still watched the ongoings of the world outside my hospital window. I felt like a an understudy watching a play. Ready and eager to play the role, yet scared and fearful to fuck up everything that seemed to be going smoothly without me.

The doctor thought I was asking her the question about my strength, "You are very strong." She grabbed my hand to give it an affectionate squeeze. The softness of her hands were a pleasant surprise. Her scent of lavender and vanilla made me warm inside. I turned to face her. She seemed to have a glow about her. To be honest usually plain white people from the Midwest were pale, milky, and cold to me. In the media they had the magic of makeup, bronzers, and spray on tans, but the doctor had a glow coming from within. Then I thought Rarely do you see that sparkle radiating from black people either.

"You just need some help. You've been through a lot that you need to deal with. I want to help you. Please tell me you will make room in your busy schedule to see me on Saturday mornings?"

It meant less rest after working late on Fridays and not being able to take a nap before going to work on Saturdays. I nodded. The doctor smiled at me proudly. She had gotten me to see things her way.

"You need to heal. Your emotions are just like a wound. Remember when you fell off your bike when you were a little girl? You would cover the scar with a Band-Aid for the first couple of days to protect it. Then when your mother would uncover it the scar would heal faster."

The doctor went on speaking as she stared in my eyes, "The scar would be ugly and exposed for everyone to see but it would heal faster. It's time for the dirty Band-Aid to come off so you can heal. With or without it everyone knows you're wounded."

I showered and put on my red strapless tube dress my mother brought to the hospital even though I instructed her to bring me my white one that reminded me of the dress Marilyn Monroe wore when her dress flew up. I knew my mother chose the red one because she always commented how she loved the color against my skin tone. I brushed my hair all back in a bun like she loved too. I drew in my sparse eyebrows and applied some gold lip gloss. As the wheel chair attendant pushed me down to the car my mother walked on my side and held my hand. Nurses, doctors, and patients gave me those same *I wonder what is wrong with her* stares or smiled sympathetically. This time I smiled back because there was nothing wrong with me.

My mother drove towards the setting sun. "Are you okay?" she asked timidly. I didn't answer for a minute. I had no idea what I was going to find when I got home. I was pretty sure that Stan was going to head for the hills after tasting a weekend of freedom. I had no idea how I was going to pay rent on my own and finish college. I would be alone. For the first time thinking those thoughts did not send me into a panic attack. I turned on the radio and Crazy in Love was playing. On cue to the beat my ass was jiggling in the car seat. *Uh oh uh oh uh oh.*

"Yeah, I'm okay or I will be."

www.ingramcontent.com/pod-product-compliance
Ingram Content Group UK Ltd.
Pitfield, Milton Keynes, MK11 3LW, UK
UKHW012055240726
13965UKWH00004B/1312

9 781257 867196